Wormwood

Wormwood

fictions by
Seán Virgo

Toronto EXILE Editions
1989

This edition is published by Exile Editions Ltd.,
69 Sullivan Street, Toronto, Ontario, Canada
M5T 1C2

Sales Distribution
General Publishing Co. Ltd.
30 Lesmill Road, Don Mills, Ontario M3B 2T6

Typeset in Century Schoolbook by TUMAX TYPESETTING COMPANY LTD.
Designed by HAROLD KURSCHENSKA
Printed by UNIVERSITY OF TORONTO PRESS

ISBN 0-920428-19-3

The publisher wishes to acknowledge the assistance towards
publication of the Canada Council and the
Ontario Arts Council.

COVER ILLUSTRATION, *"So who is Crazy Militch?"*,
by Militch of Matchva.

for my sister, Máire
"today's the day that Carthage flames tomorrow"

"And the third angel sounded, and there fell
a great star from heaven, burning as it were
a lamp, and it fell upon the third part of the
rivers and upon the fountains of waters;
And the name of the star is called Wormwood.
Apocalypse, 8 (10–11)

"You in whose ultimate madness we live,
You flinging yourself out into the emptiness,
You – like us – great an instant,

O only universe we know, forgive us."
On Frozen Fields
GALWAY KINNELL

Contents

Wormwood

Woodie

FOR JANE

WOODIE WAS ON HER KNEES by the weeping birch when she noticed a young man through the hedge, with a wheelbarrow, and she thought, Imagine that, people in the Hamilton place again, that jungle tidied up at last, and she turned back to her work, wondering how she hadn't heard that the house had been bought.

Her hands were not deft enough in the gardening gloves and she tugged them off, shifting along the cotton kneeling-pad to put them in the wicker basket with the seccateurs and the trowel and the twine.

The young man was shirtless. He was manouvering his wheel-barrow in beneath the branches of the old greengage tree.

It would be a relief, she thought, for those neglected trees, old Mr Hamilton's pride, to be cut back and cleared of some of that lichen, though late Spring was hardly the time for pruning – it would be two more years before they saw any fruit.

She began to break off the daffodil stems, tying the leaves through themselves, like topknots, the way Sonya had always insisted: so the bulbs could draw back the green life, down into themselves, for the next year. Herself, she had always wanted to leave the stems too, and allow the papery flower-husks to develop their seed-pods, but Sonya had thought they looked "trashy," standing up like that in the summer lawn. And she'd said that the effort of making seeds would deplete the bulbs' vigor. Sonya had held strong views about things like that.

The catkins were soft and yellow now – she brushed a clump of them with the back of her hand and they left a light pollen dust on her skin. She wiped it against her cheek. The buds were unseaming too – by week's end there'd be heart-shaped leaves, birth-limp and palest green, unfolding on all of the branches.

She started to hum, to be busy and content; she yearned to the little tree, well-established now after three years, its glossy trunk distinctly thicker. It would outlive her too, of course, the house would be sold, other eyes would look down from the bedroom at the trailing branches.

She concentrated on the daffodils, skirting a shudder at the thought the next owners might not keep the tree. Of all the things to fret about now!

But if it wouldn't be presumptuous, she would like to speak to that young man; or the new owners, anyway. Young men who were not professionals were so *clumsy* and enthusiastic about clearing things. The Hamilton garden was a mess, God knows – she and Sonya had slipped though the wicket gate late one evening two years ago to cut back the forsythia which was choking the beech-hedge, and found it clogged up itself with brambles and bryony vines. But the thing *was*, and she knelt up slowly, favoring her left hip and then wiping her hands on her corduroy slacks, they really should *wait* until summer had passed, they should find out what the garden contained before they went slashing and burning and cultivating, and perhaps destroying a hundred treasures.

Yes, she thought, she owed it to old Mr Hamilton to say something. She rose carefully, one knee at a time, and turned with the cotton mat in her hand towards the next daffodil patch, with its interspersed remnants of snowdrop and crocus leaves, around the dawn redwoods.

The young man had been using his wheelbarrow as a step, to reach up into the greengage. He was climbing down now and, as she walked to the lawn's end, he stood on one foot to pull off his boot. The he took off the other, and after that the grey and red socks.

Well, the young were hardy – summer was close now, but to go barefoot seemed eccentric. And who knew what nails or wire, or abandoned implements, might lurk in the matted grasses?

She could feel the smile come over her face as she knelt again, thinking of the Hamilton "mowing machines," the two sheep which he bought each year and tethered in the orchard. Each evening the old man would come down with pails of water and move the stakes, and the grass between the fruit trees was tidy as a park.

And then the roast lamb in October! Always two legs for them, a rolled breast, three or four pounds of chops.

The young man had taken off all of his clothes. He was naked and climbing back onto the barrow. Woodie hated to intrude on private acts – it would be dreadful if he should see her – and she bent as low as she could, intent on the daffodil stems. Could she possibly move away without attracting his attention?

She heard the wheelbarrow tumble, and a branch groan and creak. He must have fallen; how moritified he would feel, how doubly exposed, if he saw her now. Yet despite herself she looked over.

The young man was hanging in the greengage, his knees were bent and kicking, she could see the arms making tight, swimming motions by his face.

"Look here!" she exclaimed, and thought at once how ridiculous it was, and that she must do something. Oh dear, oh dear, but what? And she struggled up, pushing away the giddiness that swam at her eyes. She must be quick, and she made for the wicket gate, seeing as she tugged at the latch that the knees were not bent now, though the arms still clawed.

The young man's body was very pale and long. Oh dear, weren't they supposed to foul themselves when they went like that, and didn't their things stand up and, you know?

The wheelbarrow wouldn't behave, for she'd seized only one of the handles. Take hold of yourself Audrey, she thought, panic helps no one. And she righted the barrow, stepped back with it and then pushed it against the pale calves. But she was not strong enough.

"Hang on, hang on!" she cried, "I'm doing my best, we'll make it!" and she hugged the legs, which squirmed against her chest, and lifted them into the barrow. They would not take any weight and then, with a bubbling sound, the fouling did start, dribbling between the thighs.

She was crying with vexation. "Hold *on!*" she gasped, and clambered up herself into the barrow, trying so hard not to use the body as support, and then she took a huge breath and clasped the young man round his thighs, straining to lift him against the choking white rope she could see now tied to the branch.

She just hadn't the strength. A knee came up against her, she stepped back, and over the barrow went, flinging her sideways. It was an awful fall; she lay, all her breath gone, and she stared up at the twisting figure, wondering if she had broken anything. The young man's feet were white and bony and pointed downwards.

It just would not do. And the thought came – the seccateurs. There was no point looking until she got back and could be useful. Somehow she was at the gate and she was scurrying like the "little hen" Sonya used to laugh at when she hurried too much, and she flew back with the seccateurs, her plan clear, telling herself one thing only – that if the young man's thing was not standing up, then she could save him.

She got the wheelbarrow up and herself into it, feet braced on each side (she had thought of *that*, too) and reached up past the young man's face. It was livid and staring, and a horrible slip of white tongue peeped out at her. But "It'll be alright," she said, summoning authority into her breathlessness, "It'll be alright, you'll see," for his thing was not standing up, and nothing was coming from it, and though her first try with the seccateurs was blind, just a lunge and a snap overhead, it worked. The clothes line flew out and around as the young man dropped against her and backwards over the barrow where he crumpled upon himself, tipping it back on its handles, while she let go of the seccateurs and slithered across the white back, into the grass.

There was no doubt that his heart was beating, though his face was still purple and his eyes had turned eerie and white. She tugged at his arm, her hands so small they would not meet round the slack biceps, and with more luck than judgement got him securely in the wheelbarrow. One leg was bent under him and the other dangled to the grass, but he'd stayed aboard and she took that as a sign. To the house, she told herself. Come along girl, it's the only thing to do.

It took all her strength just to lift those handles and point the barrow at the gate. Alright, she told herself, eight paces at a time. Eight was her magic number.

The load was unbalanced, the grass a mass of snares, and at the gate she had to stop and go through backwards. The body slumped deeper as they went, but as the neck lolled she could see blood moving into the welt under the ears. It looked worse, but that, she assumed, was skin-deep.

It seemed to Woodie that her arms would fall off, that her back would collapse. Shamefully, a part of her started to hate this person, flaunting his nakedness at her, dragging her down so, setting her heart at a wicked trot and what's more, she saw as she paused for the twelfth time, leaving a deep rut in their lawn. If Sonya could see her now.

And the thought gave her strength, for it reminded her of the ramp they'd put in through the rockery. This was not so very much worse than the wheelchair. "We'll make it," she found herself hissing "by hook or by crook we will make it!"

But when she got to the patio she felt no achievement. She collapsed on the flags, weeping from weariness and frailty – she could just have run to the phone, as soon as she'd cut him down. "You ninny, Audrey," she said out loud, as though it were Sonya scolding, and then the young man moaned. His head went wagging from side to side and he *moaned*.

"Can you talk, can you hear me?" She pulled herself upright again with the barrow's help, "Can you hear me?" and for the first time really saw the draining features. "Why it's the Mexler boy. It's you, Daniel, isn't it?"

It seemed to her that family had moved to Toronto, some years ago. The head was still again, though a rasping noise had begun, quite regular, and the eyes had closed.

"I must phone," she said. "It's close by, I won't be a minute."

Maeterlinck got up in the rocking chair and stretched and then came running with his chirruping call. He rubbed against her arm, purring, as she dialed. No, she would not bother Dr Goodall, but if Dr Silman would call when she got back, she'd be grateful. "Audrey Woodruff, it's rather important," she said.

Back on the patio the young man's eyes rolled over and stared, but did not seem to see her. As she dragged the barrow over the sill of the French doors, Maeterlinck, belly low and tail swollen, slipped growling past her legs. It must be the smell, she thought – not just the messy thighs, but a deathroom odor she noticed now they were indoors.

Almost there. She pulled the barrow over the fawn carpet, right up to the couch, and without allowing herself any respite she got hold of the boy under his arms, pressed her thighs against the arm of the couch, and dragged him out. She banished the thought, even as it came, of what this might do to the upholstery. Then she pushed the barrow and almost flung it out of the French doors. She leant her head against the glass, took three deep breaths through the clamoring heartbeats, and turned back to the room.

Smelling salts, she remembered, and went to the armoire. The boy's face jerked away from the pungent bottle, but she kept it close to his nostrils until, with a gasp and a sob, he burst into tears and lay shivering, looking up in bewilderment.

"We must keep you warm," she said. "You just lie still," and walked through into the bathroom. She got a towel, face-cloth and blanket from the linen cupboard, pulled out a plastic bowl and went to get water at the washbasin.

A spontaneous trembling set in through her arms and shoulders. She stared at herself in the glass. The sixty-four year old face, with its brief frame of iron-grey hair, wore the woeful expression she remembered from when she was eight or nine. And still, across her cheek, a yellow smudge of birch pollen.

She cleaned the boy up as thoroughly as she could, gently tugging his hand away when he tried to cover himself. He began weeping again.

"Do you think you could walk?" she asked "There's a bed just through that door." He tried to get up, and succeeded with her help. His breath was loud and sour. She wrapped the blanket round his shoulders and led him by the arm to the study-bedroom. "I'll get your clothes from the orchard," she said. "You just try to sleep, Daniel. You are Daniel, aren't you?" He nodded again, his eyes were shot with blood. "Just rest, sleep if you can. I have called Dr Silman."

The doctor's car drove in about six o'clock and Woodie hastened up from the laundry to let her in. Impatient of all but essentials, the young doctor could be brusque in ways that Woodie would have found rude in anyone else.

"You alright, Woodie?" she said and walked straight on into the living room.

"It was good of you to come at this hour, Emma – I know the girls will be hungry."

The doctor shifted her bag to her left hand. "If I didn't give then an excuse to eat junk food twice a week and feel neglected, they'd fire me," she said. "Well, where'd you put him?" Woodie gestured and the doctor squeezed her arm briefly and then said in a public voice "Let's see what the little shmuck has to say for himself." Woodie's "Do be gentle with him –" was addressed to the closing door.

Woodie went back to the basement to put Daniel's clothes in the dryer and the sofa cushion-covers in the wash. She admired Emma Silman's spunk and energy, her moving out to the country with two young girls, and all her work with the chamber orchestra, as well as her patients.

Woodie wondered if you could put running shoes in the dryer. She decided against it – they still smelled revolting and they were coming apart. I will buy him some clothes, she thought.

She could hear Emma's voice upstairs, softening now from the first staccato announcements. Was she being gentle enough? But if you can trust anyone, she reminded herself, it is Emma Stilman. In that same study-bedroom the doctor had sat down with them and said "Okay, you're both grown up girls, so I'm not going to pussyfoot." And explained that for her, medicine had to do with the quality of life, not its prolongation. "Modern medicine, the billions of research dollars, is mostly a matter of diminishing returns. That's why I moved here. That and the dreary shlemiel of a husband I found myself stuck with!"

Woodie had sat between grief and shock and a certain prim disapproval, but Sonya had laughed.

"Drugs? Oh sister will I prescribe you drugs! First marijuana to keep up your appetite, and then when we're beyond that, you get heroin so you can stay good and stoned and enjoy the world you're preparing to leave. All three of us will be committing a felony. Okay?"

She had come twice a day, and had learned their language at once. "Men are such cowards," she announced, drawing the fluid into a hypodermic," it's always the woman who winds up taking it on the chin!"

And another time, "Woodie, the world needs people like you, but God you'd make a lousy mess of running it!" Sonya had loved her.

Woodie was waiting for the doctor in the living room, with cake and madeira. "He won't try it again," was the loud verdict, before she had closed the door behind her. "And there's no real damage, only bruising and a kinked sterno mastoid. He can breathe, that's what counts, though he won't be talking much. I doubt very much that that's a great loss!"

She drank her wine standing. "Now, this notion of yours. I'm only concerned about you Woodie – you're by far the more valuable patient." She used Woodie's murmur of protest as a springboard for her next declaration.

"Okay, this would be far better for him than the alternatives.

The city, which he can't hack, clinics, therapy, his family. And he won't get out of line with you, this I guarantee. But –" and her voice softened, though her direct gaze was hardly gentle, "– do you want the intrusion?"

Woodie said "Yes."

"Alright, then," the doctor was at the door already. "Rest, lots to drink, no milk for the first day. A little bit of attention, on *your* terms. I'll come round tomorrow."

As she got to her car: "Might be good for you, Woodie."

"I think so," she murmured.

And just before driving off: "Don't expect too much, Woodie – the kid's a loser. I doubt like hell if he's got a thought in his head."

The car left a wake if energy in the driveway. And Woodie guessed that the last words were a challenge.

Woodie heard Daniel get up and go to the bathroom during the night. It was something she hadn't thought of; she was relieved. She spent the following day in the garden, out of his way, but she visited him periodically to replenish his jugs of apple juice and water, and in the evening brought him a light turkey broth. He did not speak, except to say "Thank you" each time, in a whisper. He seemed completely, sometimes tearfully, misplaced. But he did look better.

Even when she looked at the damage, to the lawn and the carpet, she was satisfied. A turn of events it was, she thought, to be nursing someone back to life here, instead of away from it.

Next morning she walked into town and bought clothes for Daniel, replacing as closely as possible the ones he'd been wearing, for she did not want him to feel uncomfortable. But she did buy two roll-neck jerseys, so he might hide his neck.

In the Algonquin Tea Rooms she suddenly had a scheme. She went back to the menswear store and bought work boots and gloves for him.

And then she bought so many groceries that she had to arrange for them to be delivered.

As she came up the back lane she heard the bass thudding of loud music and, close to the house, realised he was playing the radio at full volume. Maeterlinck cowered in the rhododendrons and would not come out. It was unbearable inside, she could feel the house plants cringing. Oh their music – it was as jarring and incomprehensible as the language they used, quite casually, in the Main Street. The girls too. Some young man, she assumed, with a strangled voice, was wailing *You know what it's like to be aloh-oh-ohne* as she threw the door open to the study-bedroom, and put her hands to her ears.

He was out of bed, sitting in the armchair right next to the radio, a totally vacant expression on his face. He did not see her till she waded through the barrage gesturing at him. He scrambled up and turned the radio off. "Sorry," he said and then, seeing her expression more clearly, "I'm honestly sorry." His look was utterly stricken. "Dr Silman put the fear of God into you, didn't she?" Woodie said, and was privately grateful. "Well never mind – you're getting your voice back, and I'm sure this is a sign of progress. Now sit down *please*." And when he had: "Now, Daniel, this has always been a very quiet house. By all means play the radio, but softly, please."

"I *am* sorry," he said, "Miss Woodruff."

"Woodie – everyone calls me Woodie."

She called Maeterlinck through the open window. He came chirruping round the house, but did not jump up to the sill. "I'm going to make some tea," she told Daniel, "and I'll scramble some eggs and see if I can tempt you. Then we have things to talk about – I've had an idea." She felt quite mysterious though he, she noticed, looked merely apprehensive.

He was not an attractive boy. He did not seem *clean*, somehow. There was a dark down on his upper lip that you could not call a moustache, and an awkward chin. His hair was lank, and he was a mouthbreather, unless that was because of his accident. Charity, Audrey, she told herself. And he did have gentle eyes, with fine, long lashes.

She coaxed Maeterlinck in through the window, and he accepted some egg from Daniel's fork. "Where'd you get that name from?" the boy asked. Woodie laughed: "It's a joke of ours. A little revenge against a great man who hated cats."

"I don't mind them," said Daniel.

He was tonguetied when she laid his new clothes on the bed. He was so passive to everything that happened or was given to him, as though he came from a world with no values or rituals whatsoever.

"Do you have a driver's licence?" she asked.

"Sure. But I got no car; I couldn't afford the insurance."

"Well, this is my plan. I haven't been up to our cottage for three years now – someone does go in every Fall, but it must be a terrible mess. I thought you might like to drive up there with me and help me set the place to rights. You'd be doing me a great favor and I would, of course, pay you for your labors."

"What kind of car you got?" he asked.

She was a little nonplussed. "Why – it's a Studebaker. I can drive, of course, but don't enjoy it. Mrs Hansen always did the driving."

"You don't mean that grey Studebaker, you had when we lived here?"

"Yes, that's right. It's been very well looked after."

"That's great," he said, and he was actually animated. "When do we go?"

"We mustn't rush things," she said. She could not suppress her smile. "Just maybe the day after tomorrow."

"Why not tomorrow?"

"Oh I don't think you'd be up to it so soon –"

"I would, for sure, Miss Woodie. Let's go tomorrow."

Miss Woodie! "Alright," she said.

He drove importantly but with care through the outskirts of town, and Woodie told herself to relax. The trunk and back seat were filled with groceries, and Maeterlinck, who had always travelled well, was already asleep on a box of towels and toilet paper.

Woodie took out her writing-case and put on her reading glasses.

"These old cars were sure built comfortable," Daniel said. He patted the leather arm-rest. "How come you only got 34,000 miles on her?"

"We did not drive very much," she said, taking off her glasses from politeness. His adam's apple was prominent over the beige roll-neck. "The only real journeys we made were to the cottage and then, in September, to Niagara-on-the-Lake." She turned back to her letters.

Daniel reached for the radio: "You don't mind eh?" "Well –" she said, and took off her glasses again, but he smiled: "Don't worry, Miss Woodie – I'll find something you'll like."

"Just so long," she said firmly, "as there are no commercials. Those I find a real intrusion on my life." The young seemed so afraid of stillness, of silence, she thought. Perhaps everyone was, nowadays. But, she supposed, there was so much noise and clutter everywhere, perhaps they had to block some of it out.

After five or six alarming bursts of popular programming, he settled on something that might, she thought, be Prokofiev.

"Why thank you, Daniel."

"You bet," he said. "Those classical guys are real musicians eh?"

He beat his fingers on the wheel, as if conjuring a backbeat from the orchestra, and just north of Chesley she realised that the car had picked up speed. The needle was approaching 70.

She touched his arm. "This car has never in its life gone faster than fifty miles per hour, Daniel, and I am not impressed by speed."

Such a look of dismay came over him, and the car slowed so suddenly, that she was quite alarmed. "Now, now," she said, "I'm not that fierce, am I?" But he was pulling the car over. Behind them, lights flashing, a patrol car was stopping too.

Daniel sat numbly, his face averted, till the policeman stood by the window. "Licence please," he said, "Don't you read the signs?" As Daniel fumbled in his pocket, the policeman peered in at Woodie. His manner changed noticeably. "Officer," Woodie said, "this young man is kindly driving me up to Star Lake. It is my car and he's not quite used to it yet."

The policeman's eyes moved from hers back to Daniel. "That's no excuse for speeding," he said. "30 kilometers over the limit. I'd be more careful if I had a lady aboard."

Daniel's plastic wallet held nothing but his licence, a social security card and a few scraps of paper. "Alright," said the officer, "bring the registration back to my car. This won't take long, ma'am," he added, "so long as he's not in our computer.

But as Daniel opened the door, Maeterlinck slipped past him, under the car and out of sight.

A minute later, the three of them were standing by the ditch calling vainly and parting the horsetails and last year's tangle of grass. There was no sign of the cat until Daniel, wandering twenty yards back from the police car, suddenly whooped "He's here, I got him, Miss Woodie," and plunged into the ditch. When they came up: "He went in there," he said, crestfallen, pointing to a culvert pipe. "You scared him, shouting like that," said the officer, and as Daniel's eyes dropped, Woodie saw a more thoughtful look cross the policeman's face.

How strange it was, she thought, how strange men were, that as soon as they could feel pity for someone their assertiveness left them. They could afford to be gentle.

Daniel went over the road and down in the other ditch. "He's in there!" he yelled, part of his voice echoing under the road, "I'll chase him through!"

"Take it easy," called the officer, "don't scare him!" and he climbed down to the culvert.

Policemen were the first to look young, Sonya had often said, policemen and soldiers. After that, doctors and bank-managers, and when you began to see young priests you knew you were "over the hill." But it was the young in uniform, Woodie thought, who were the most upsetting.

The policeman had put his hat, and Daniel's licence in it, on the culvert's projecting lip. He grinned up: "I noticed that old Studebaker of yours, you've kept it in fine shape," and then, "Here he comes," he said, and scooped Maeterlinck up from the mouth of the culvert. He climbed up to the road and handed the purring cat back to its mistress. "Don't worry," he said, as he retrieved his hat, "I'm not going to give him a ticket."

Woodie beamed: "You are a gentleman," she said, and noticed with some surprise that he received her compliment as if it were a medal.

Daniel emerged, his new clothes rucked and muddy, his hair awry. He smiled at Woodie uncertainly. The officer handed back his licence. "Off you go now," he said, "and make sure you don't give this lady any more trouble."

Daniel's clothes were in far worse shape by the end of the day. He went with abandon at the young poplars which had sprung up down the centre of the trail, all over the rough lawn, up against the side porch and across the path to the dock. He used the old *parang* Woodie's father had brought from Indonesia, and made a huge pile of the branches beside the boatshed. Daniel had never heard of poplars, he called them "populars," while Woodie, though she disliked their promiscuous growth and their uselessness as firewood or timber, felt a pang as she saw so many of them slaughtered. And there was no denying that a mature poplar carried wonderful, whispered mysteries when a summer breeze moved through its leaves.

There were other slaughters. Maeterlinck had a count of three deermice and a fox-squirrel by sundown, and when Woodie had tidied the chaos those animals had made of her cupboards, she set out a dozen traps. "I'll move the bodies," Daniel told her. She laughed. "That's very thoughtful," she said, "but I am a country girl and have never been thought squeamish."

But regularly, through the night, she heard the snap of one trap after another.

Next morning he was still asleep two hours after she had risen. She washed the counters and floors, and cleared sugar-mold off the jars of preserves, and then went for a walk round the old place before making breakfast and bringing it to him in bed. From then on he got up as early as she did.

It took two days before the cottage felt like home again, days of open windows and constant fires before the smell of damp and neglect began to evaporate. Daniel was almost invisible; he seemed quite content to sit on the side porch by himself, when he was not working, and in a way Woodie was put out that he accepted everything so passively. Not once did he comment on the cottage or the furnishings, the rugs, the great stone fireplace, all the lesser treasures – the books, pictures and local trophies – that she and Sonya had gathered to this place over twenty summers. But he worked with a will, there was no denying that.

They were almost the first people up at the lake. They heard only two boats and at night there were no lights except across at the Delwisch place. Woodie got back to her old routine, working on her correspondence in the mornings, swimming in the afternoons, though the lake was still chilly and the waterweed, she found, had invaded whole stretches of the shallows.

Daniel chopped wood and cleared brush, swept the porches and cleaned out the gutters. He even, inefficiently, cleaned the big windows: "You should have one of them windshield things they have at gas stations," he said, when the sun came round to the west and showed up the streaks and patches on the glass. At noon on the fourth day he came up to the back-porch, drenched and shivering, to say he had fixed the dock. The stone-crib it rested on had been shifted by ice and the deck had canted impossibly, but he had been in the water for two hours, moving the stones, and at the expense of a gashed foot and three bruised fingers, he had set it to rights.

"Good for you," Woodie cried warmly, and put down her work and prescribed a bath and hot buttered rum.

They went down to the dock later on, and she swam while he nailed back boards that had come adrift. "You know," she called out, treading water, "I do believe you've filled out since you came here." He grinned and flexed his biceps. "And your skin," she said, "it has caught the sun." She bobbed under water and came closer: "You should cover up, some of the time; you don't want to burn."

"What about you Miss Woodie – you've been outside as much as me."

She paddled over to the dock and worked her elbows onto it. She felt younger than she had in years. "Oh the sun's never bothered me," she said. "My father used to say there must be some Indian blood on my mother's side – we all turned brown as berries in a week."

That night, after supper, they sat by the fireplace and drank plum wine, while the radiogram played old favorites of hers and Sonya's – "Liebsleid," Haydn's flute pieces, "The Hebrides" – and the cherry wood logs, cut four years before, consumed themselves fiercely. For the first time, as gently as possible, she asked him about the "accident." "I don't like to pry," she told him, "but I would like to understand."

He stared at his drink, and the fire. "There's nothing to understand," he said. "I had no reason to," and drank some wine and grimaced, "I'd no reason not to, either. I talked about it a bit to that doctor."

"I'm sorry," she said, "I didn't know. It's just so bewildering to see a young person –" "I wouldn't try it again," he broke in, "The doctor told you that."

The baroque flute played out its ordered course, Maeterlinck purred on her lap. "Why the Hamilton's orchard?" she whispered; if he didn't hear perhaps it was just as well. Woodie felt impertinent.

"I just remembered it. When we were kids. We used to play there, and steal apples. We stole your apples too." "And our cherries." "That's right. A couple of times we watched you at the window, after dark. Mrs Hansen used to brush your hair."

"Oh dear," she said sadly, "when you look out at the darkness, you see only your own reflections."

In the morning she told him he'd earned a rest. Would he like to go into Owen Sound and mail her letters for her? He accepted the fifty dollars she gave him, without comment. He was itching to get to the car, but before he left he told her, with a whole new air about him, "I was thinking you shouldn't go swimming when I'm away. Like, suppose you caught a charleyhorse and there'd be no one there to help?"

"That's very thoughtful of you, Daniel," she said, "but, you know, even young people may catch cramps. But I will be careful."

He carried the pile of correspondence out to the car. "What do you write all these letters for, Miss Woodie? What's this *OWL* on the envelopes?"

"I am secretary this year for a society," she said, rather formally. "It is the One World League, and our final aim," and felt a light blush come up at the pretentious sound, "is world government, you see."

"Yeah, that makes sense," he said. "Sort of like ..."

"Yes?"

"Oh nothing. Go on." She could see him wanting to talk, but he held back, afraid of his thoughts being wrong. Or his words being wrong, which was almost the same thing.

"Well, I won't make a speech. But we have members in more than forty countries, and I have made so many friends in the last three years, I can hardly keep up. Now off you go, and enjoy yourself. I'll have supper ready at seven, and it's to be a special one."

"No don't stop, Miss Woodie, I like you to talk. I never heard anyone talk like you, even teachers. It's like you talk in whole sentences, like it was written down."

"Well, thank you for that," she laughed. "Words should be our servants you know," and laughed again: "I suppose that is just what you meant!"

"Yeah."

"Well anyway, Daniel, our whole belief is that if you think the best of people, they will behave at their best. And that is the way we write to the leaders in less fortunate countries. Now you take that car for a drive."

"No one ever called me Daniel before," he said. "I like it, coming from you."

"I guess no one ever called me Miss Woodie, either. And I like it too."

As she walked down to the dock she thought, he is a dear boy at heart, but she thought too, what he probably feared is that I'd have a heart attack. And of course, as soon as she heard the car out on the road, she plunged in the water, because now she could swim undressed, as they always had. But for Daniel's sake she stayed within her depth.

She floated on her back, watching the marsh hawks cruising the reed beds, listening to the small birds everywhere, and she thought that though this solitude was a relief, it would make sense to keep Daniel around for a while, if he wished. To pay him would be no problem, for Sonya's insurance was all in Government Bonds, breeding money, and could be withdrawn at need. It would be good for both of them, she told herself.

He got back at 6.30, she'd begun to worry, came running in from the front porch and thrust a great parcel at her. "This is for you, Miss Woodie," and stood, eyes fixed on her face. "Go on!" He could hardly control his excitement. It was a picture, she could tell, the first thing she saw was the price on the brown-paper backing: $34.95, reduced from $65. It was a ghastly, impasto landscape, of a cottage and birchtrees, a lake and two deer in the foreground, "Oh Daniel," she faltered, and then, determinedly cried "We shall hang it on the chimney breast – it has always needed a picture. And it will remind me that you have been here."

And then he said, "Guess what, Miss Woodie? I've enlisted."

"Enlisted?"

"Yeah, the forces. They'll train me, and send me to school if I want, and I'll get to travel all over."

"Oh," she said. "Well, Daniel, my uncle was a soldier, and he was a gentleman."

"We keep the peace, you know, Miss Woodie."

"Indeed you do," she said heatedly, "and we are very proud of you."

"Yeah."

"But, Daniel – your neck."

"Yeah, I thought of that. I don't have to get my medical for two weeks, it'll be alright by then, won't it?"

"I should think so," she said. "Now you get washed up, and we'll eat."

He talked all through the meal, she could scarcely believe this was the same boy. Gabbling and gobbling at the same time. She had read in so many novels about mothers and grandmothers delighting in "healthy animal appetites" but had not really believed it. She was always rather fastidious about food. But he was so happy. "It'll be good for me," he said wisely, "sort of like being here with you, and work, and a routine and all that." Relax, Audrey, and share his pleasure, she told herself. And she did.

He built a huge fire while she prepared the earthenware jug, pouring a bottle and a half of red bordeaux over the sachet of spices, then dropping two sticks of cinnamon in. She placed it by the hearth and then thrust the "cutlass" deep into the fire. "Mulled wine," she announced. "It is a tradition in this house on Friday nights. We shall probably both end up quite tipsy!"

They stared at the flames for ten minutes; she had Schnabel's "Pathetique" playing softly on the radiogram. And then, with mock formality, she withdrew the "cutlass."

"You look like a soldier yourself, Miss Woodie."

"Why yes," she cried, seeing not herself, but Sonya, with the "cutlass" *en garde*, and she giggled, "I suppose I do," and she plunged the poker's fading tip into the jug.

Was she being selfish, she wondered, as the soft fumes of the wine crept up in her; should she have let him go on as he was instead of creating this ritual, with herself in control? No, it would be something for him to remember. And having him there made it easier for her to continue the old routine.

She turned the record over, "The Moonlight," and got down the Treasury from the inglenook shelf. "Now I'll read to you for a while, Daniel," as she sat back in the rocking chair. "Mulled wine and good music and poetry, in the heart of the wilderness."

She read him "The Listeners," "The Retreate," "Stopping by Woods on a Snowy Evening" and "A Narrow Fellow in the Grass," taking her time, giving each word its value but intoning less, she realised, than was Sonya's taste. The piano continued; she went and ladled more wine into their goblets. She smiled brightly, not wanting to ask.

"I liked that first one," he said, "about the haunted house."

"'The Listeners' – *But only a host of phantom listeners*
             That dwelt in the lone house then –" –

"Yeah, and when he knocks at the door –"

"'*Tell them I came, and no one answered*
    That I kept my word' he said ..."

and she recited the ending to him:

   "*Ay they heard his foot on the stirrup*
    And the sound of iron upon stone
    And how the darkness surged softly backwards
    When the plunging hooves were gone."

and felt that she had left magic hanging in the room. "Walter de la Mare," she said in a moment. "It is, I believe, an almost perfect poem. Perhaps – ," well, why not, "Perhaps you'd like to read me one, Daniel?"

He fumbled through the pages as though handling a book were as great a mystery as holding a baby. "'Goblin Market'?" he said at last, "What's that like?"

"Oh not that!" she cried, for the poem's ending was her and Sonya's romance. "It's – rather long," she explained.

"Do you write poetry, Miss Woodie?"

"Why no," she said, "though I dreamed of doing so when I was young."

"But isn't this your writing?" He held a slip of paper, one of the many that marked places in the Treasury. "*'Why do you look at the world through glass?'*" he read, doubtfully.

"Oh, let me see –" and she crossed the hearth to look down over his shoulder. There were five lines in Sonya's handwriting. Woodie replaced her glasses: on the printed page, Frances Cornford's "To a Lady Seen from a Train:"

> *O why do you walk through the fields in gloves,*
> *Missing so much and so much?*
> *O fat white woman who nobody loves,*
> *Why do you walk through the fields in gloves,*
> *.....................*
> *Missing so much and so much?*

Sonya's poem read:

> *O why do you look at the world through glass,*
> *Missing so much and so much?*
> *O smug young poet, you smirk as you pass,*
> *But why do you look at the world through glass,*
> *Missing so much and so much?*

That was Sonya, tart, witty, indignant. "It is Mrs Hansen's poem," said Woodie, "and very clever too." She looked in the jug. "Why, the wine is cooled, and almost finished anyway. What would you say to another jug?" "Oh sure," said Daniel. "It's good."

Woodie took the jug, and the book, into the kitchen. "Just stick the 'cutlass' back in the fire, would you?" she called.

"The cutlass? Sure, okay."

Woodie had never seen the poem in that way; it had, in fact, been a favorite of hers,

> *When the grass is soft as the breast of doves*
> *And shivering sweet to the touch,*
> *O why do you walk through the fields in gloves,*

but Sonya who, it must be admitted, had grown junoesque in the three years before illness struck, was perhaps sensitive.

There it sat, like a note from the other side. Unmistakably Sonya.

Perhaps, Woodie thought, she had been meant to find it when she was alone, or "single again" as brave Sonya had insisted on saying. Was it another reminder to her dear Audrey, of what she'd so often said: "People see what suits *them*, Audrey, and what suits them will certainly not take *you* into account." Perhaps she *did* try too hard to agree with people, perhaps she *did* sometimes realise afterwards that she had been imposed upon. But even Sonya, she knew, protective as she was, found Woodie's weaknesses lovable.

They finished the second jug of hot wine and were, indeed, quite tipsy. Woodie at last said "Goodnight, dear," and left him by the fire, happy, and probably imagining great deeds in his new life.

As she came through from the bathroom, she saw that the sky and the lake were ablaze with white flames. The Lights. She hurried across the bedroom and pulled the window wide, and watched as the great white draperies of the northern sky unfolded and closed, whispering and crackling across the night. Sonya had thought them angels' wings, though she had never been able to hear their song.

She wanted to be out with them. The walls of her room, even the flyscreen, separated her from them. And, Daniel must see them, she thought, and slipped through the screen door to stand for a moment, barefoot on the boards, hugging her peignoir around her, and watching. Up by the driveway an owl called repeatedly: *Hoo, hoo, hoo-hoo, hoo-hoo-hoo*. The lake breeze played upon her neck and her wrists.

Then she went on down the porch to find Daniel. He was not in the living room, but where the light spilled in through the study door, she saw him.

She moved close to the window. He was stretched out in the armchair, his face lolling back, she could see his adam's apple rise. Sonya's photograph of her was on his raised knee and he held his flesh, running his hand up and down on it brutally.

All this in the moment before she tapped on the window. He doubled over, but she could see he had stopped too late and she stood mutely, looking through the glass as he bolted from the room. A moment later she heard his feet on the front porch.

She went in, averting her eyes from the chair, and retrieved her photo. He had thrown it down, but the glass had not broken. She hugged it to her, and carried it out through the living room. The lamplight caught a streak of moisture down its centre and she saw, as she held it out, a milky tear where the glass met the frame.

She rushed to the bathroom, cleaned off the glass with a tissue, and stood with it held to her breast, rigid with shock and outrage, staring through her image in the mirror.

She said, out loud, "I hate his picture, I hate his clothes and his hanging mouth, I hate his stupid penis, I hate the smell of his feet, he *defiles* me."

In the photograph, she lay beneath the wild plum tree, naked upon the grass, just her face in the fretted shade of a fern-spray. Their first summer, before the porches were built or the dock repaired. Their romance.

The Lights were still playing through her bedroom window. I just wanted him to be happy, she thought, and almost heard Sonya's voice: "Wishing people happiness is to condescend to them, Audrey. Wish them to *grow*."

The front door was open. She went out on the porch. "Daniel," she called, softly. Then much louder: "Daniel, please come back in. Please." The frogs were clamoring down by the reedbeds, the early spring squeaking calls. The crackle of the lights merged with their voices. "Daniel?"

She moved to the rail and leant her knuckles upon it. "I believe," she said loudly, to him, to the night, "that the physical act is the loneliest thing in the world."

It was true. Sonya's always gentle but overwhelming gusts of passion were aberrations from the harmony of their life. The disposition of a room, the scheduled pattern of the garden, the girlish excitement of the chapter awaiting them each evening, from "Kristin Lavransdatter," "Mist over Pendle" or "Lord of the Rings." The sharing of parts each time they read "The Bluebird" and Sonya's sly joke upon Materlinck, who has so feared all cats. But passion, she had learned, always died where it fell. It was as though Sonya had wanted to lose herself, to believe the worst of herself. And then there was a gap, a healing to be made.

Maeterlinck chirruped to her left, and when she looked down she saw him among the irises, by the feet of Daniel, who cowered against the cottage wall.

He did not look up; he hugged his knees and stared out. "Oh Daniel," she said, "There are things that I don't understand, more than you can imagine, but I do try."

And when he did not respond, she said, "Please come in. I want you to know that we can simply forget this happened. I was only so angry because that photograph of me was very precious, it came from a precious time."

"That was you, Miss Woodie?"

"Yes, of course."

"Oh god," he muttered, "oh god."

"Didn't you realise that?"

"Of course not," and he stood up, his head level with her knees, but did not meet her eyes. "You were so pretty."

A host of little hands tried to beat him away inside her mind, but she overrode them. "It was a blessed time, Daniel," she said. "Now I think you should really get to bed."

There was only one thing for it, she decided, back in her bedroom, she should have "a good cry." And softly, pleasure and relief began to unlock in her. Woodie permitted herself tears only at very long intervals. Sonya's "good cries" had been weekly retreats, but for Woodie it wasn't so simple. She had to feel sure she had earned it.

But it was creeping up through her now. And she *had* earned it. Woodie, she told herself, you have earned it. Get on with it.

She moved her pillows to the foot of the bed and lay on her stomach, her face practically on the windowsill. The water was still, the frogs had quietened down, there was only the dwindling tremor of the Lights behind the trees.

Woodie wept, voluptuously, loudly, and for at least ten minutes. She wept for Sonya, for loneliness, for her own bright determination, as she had not wept for two years. Halfway through, with an impulsive jerk, she pulled the window wide open, without a thought for her cries in the room next door or across the water.

In that surrender was so much joy and sorrow comingled that when she pushed the top pillow away, drenched as it was, she fell instantly asleep, and slept without dreams or movement till the sun was high over the trees.

She turned onto her back, and fondled Maeterlinck's ears, and listened to the sound of an axe splitting firewood near the driveway.

Wormwood

T HE VOICES OF MAN fall through the forest.

They are like the yelping of crows, but they ricochet and fade, aimless among the trees.

The forest conspires against them. It seems to go on but it is holding its breath, waiting for them to pass. The place locks into itself; it becomes a huge, decaying room, filmed with damp molds, stifling in its own inert odours.

The kinglets and chickadees that cry and forage overhead are ghosts on an empty stage, they embroider the scenery. In the ears of Man they are bells and jews' harps, high in the branches of hemlocks and amabilis firs.

The eyes of Man see them flit, like swift dark butterflies, where the fans and sheaves of hemlock and cedar foliage almost shut out the sky.

The voices of Man are unnaturally loud, making no echo, cut off at the moment of utterance.

Over a broken rock-face the roots fall, exposed, crisscrossing each other.

The boy came down at a run, leaping the last six feet from the root-ladder, and landed, gasping and laughing, by the little stream.

There was a patch of gravel, water swirling around it like beer, with spindrifts of foam, and the sudden pounce of sunlight through a gap in the branches.

The boy threw himself down on the bank and shrugged his rucksack free. He eased off his sneakers and rummaged behind him for one of the bottles. The twist-cap spun away into the salal thicket past an old cedar stump, and the boy dug his toes into the gravel, drank deeply from his bottle and lay back in the patch of sunlight.

His girl was halfway down the network of roots on the rock-face, coming down backwards, each foot blind and timid as it reached for support. "You might give me a hand!" she called down.

The boy smiled and leaned up on one elbow. "You've made it this far," he said, and swigged at his bottle. "You've done great – you shouldn't ask for help now!"

"My legs aren't as long as yours!"

His eyes scanned her leg, from the muddied sneaker groping at the roots, up to the line of her shorts.

"You have a wonderful ass," he said, and got up to go to her help. But she jumped the last few feet and turned, leaning against the rock face, panting. Her face was uniformly pink, with sweat at her hairline and her eyebrows. Her sunglasses were still propped up, on the top of her head. "Bastard!" she said.

"Want a drink?" he held out the bottle.

"In a minute. I want to taste that water first."

"It'll be pretty rank," he said, "coming out through those roots and all that rotting stuff."

"No," the girl said, "you're wrong. Look how clear it is, like amber in the sunlight. It'll be like drinking the forest."

He laughed: "Help yourself – at least it won't be polluted."

But the girl stood, now she had caught her breath, and sniffed. "God, it's primitive here," she said. "What's the smell – that musky smell?"

"Skunk cabbage, I guess."

"Smells like bear to me."

"You ever smell a bear?"

"No," she said. "This is the first time!"

"Hah! It's skunk cabbage, don't worry."

"I'm not worried – I'd love to see a bear. But it *is* primitive."

"I guess ... No, I'd just say it was wild."

"Primitive. It's like – listen," she held one finger up towards his lips. "I can hear it – it's a heart beating in the forest. No, listen. Can you hear?"

They were still for a moment; the girl closed her eyes.

"Yes, I hear what you mean. Strange, eh?" He drank from the bottle again. "But that's your own heart, isn't it? – the blood in your ears after scrambling down here."

The girl's eyes opened and she smiled at him. "I think you're right. But, hey –" and she moved past him, brushing his thigh with her hand, "– maybe that's what I meant. Hearing your heartbeat in the trees. That's primitive: when things are so still."

The girl knelt, lowering her face almost to the stream's surface, and drank from her cupped hands, scooping up water too over her face and her throat, and into the open neck of her shirt.

"Don't move! Stay that way!" The boy put down his beer and pulled a camera from the rucksack, splashing across the gravel bar and over to the other bank.

"What d'you want?"

"It's terrific," he said, "just hold it. You look like the Fly Woman, with those shades on the top of your head."

"I forgot they were there," the girl's hand went up, instinctively, to her hair, "and thanks a lot anyway: first it's a beer commercial and now you've got a horror movie?"

"No, no," the boy juggled his light meter and the camera lens. "I've got a great view of your boobs too. Hold it!"

"You always take so long," she said. "It gets too self-conscious, and look – I cant stay like this, I have to go to the bathroom."

The boy took a picture, shifted a bit to the right and took another.

"We're short on bathrooms," he said, "but go ahead – just pee downstream, alright?"

"I don't need to *pee*." The girl scrambled up and clutched her midriff. "It's always like this when I get into the woods. Something goes loose inside."

The boy waded back through the stream. "It's funny," he said, and touched her arm, "the same thing happens to me when I go into a library." He knelt by his rucksack as she walked off, pushing through a gap in the salal beside the cedar stump.

The boy changed the lens on his camera and began to focus on different things around him: the roots on the rock face, a glistening spray of huckleberry leaves, the half-exposed gravels in the sunlight. He knelt by the water and stared through his camera's eye at the stream bed.

The girl pushed through to the end of the thicket. There was a trail of some kind, though very faint; there was an axe-blaze on a dead alder trunk and she could see, up ahead, a tag of blue surveyor's tape on a branch. But she turned aside where the rock-face opened to a narrow cleft, arched over with salal and fallen trees, with the sound of water trickling. She went in and leaned against the stone, bracing her legs as best she could, and then pushed her shorts and pants free, releasing herself a second later.

The dampness and cold of the stone pushed through her shirt against her shoulder blades. Clusters of fern poked from every crack in the rock, and the whole place was furred with moss. She felt almost submerged.

She stripped handfulls of moss from the wall beside her, wondering how long it would take to grow back. It was cold and velvety on her fingers, but after the first chill it scratched a little when she wiped herself. She made a little pile of it over her leavings and wondered now how long it would take for those traces of her, unevenly clinging to the nap of the moss, to get absorbed by the forest.

The boy was focussing his camera on the cedar stump. It was capped with an emerald moss-pad, so that you could not tell if it had been cut by man or had simply died. In the lens's close-up he saw the miniature forest of moss as his eyes would never have: orange and crimson elf-caps stood up at him, the mats and curlicues beneath them were an endless labyrinth. The scale of things made him almost dizzy.

The girl came back through the thicket. "There's a trail," she said, "not much of one, but it's clear. I wonder who made it."

"Trapper maybe," he said. "Hold still, I want a close up of your face."

The girl took off her sunglasses and laid them on the mossy stump. "They don't allow trapping in a park, do they?" The sunglasses slipped off the moss and down into the salal. "Hold it," the boy said, and clicked the shutter twice. "Must be a warden, then. We should follow it, it'll probably take us out by the beach." He stepped closer and focussed again. "You've got moss and twigs in your hair," he said. "I've got moss and twigs everywhere," she laughed, and pushed past him to the stream bank. She pulled off her sneakers, then her shorts and pants, and sat on the gravel bar. "Aaah!" she sighed, "I like this place."

"It'll be cold soon," the boy said, "the sun's almost left us. Shall we take that trail?"

"Sure," the girl said, "but just give me a minute, okay?"

The boy stalked her with the camera, his feet in the water. Close-ups of her profile, of her hand loose over her knee, of her feet on the stream bed. He moved up her thighs and focussed on her crotch. In the amber refracted light, set off by the pallor of her thighs, it was like a sea-organism, an anenome, the light-brown tendrils lifted by the stream's flow, the pale flesh-hood just a hint. The girl reached back to get the beer bottle from beside his rucksack. "Oh don't move," he whispered. "Come back."

He put down the camera and stared, fascinated by what his eyes knew but could not see. The girl held her breath, the bottle halfway to her lips.

The raw message was triggered in the boy's belly; his face lifted and the girl's eyes were kindled by his. Her look was like fear, but it was eager: she put down the bottle beside her in the shallows as the boy found himself lunging through the water on his knees, tugging his shorts free with one hand as he reached for her waist with the other.

The voices of Man collide and merge. The barks and whines of pain or appetite, the mounting breath. The water churns as it does when the fish come, under the winter stars, to spawn. They are death cries, the drawn out rasps of something coming to an end.

Behind the cedar stump, as far into the shadows as the thing which held her would allow, She lay and endured. Her breath was stilled against pain and the voices of Man, but She could not still her heart as the forest did. She was being separated by the different fears and messages. Pain taught her stillness, so did the yelps and smells and stumblings of Man and all the fierce odors of altered things which came with them.

But the thing which gripped her leg was an altered thing too, its bite inert and relentless. Her heart commanded her to fight it loose and to get away from it. And across those commands came little surges from her stomach, where her breasts continued to fill and leak despite her, calling her away from herself. Patience, which was her essence, had become a torture.

The huge blank eyes that had dropped by her hiding place, stared in at her and reflected her misery.

When at length the white limbs came trampling by her through the salal, and the voices of Man receded like the low mockery of gulls, and the stream shouted and clamoured as it had before, She came back into the open. At once the thing tore at her leg again and the pain flattened her to the earth.

It did not chew or tug. After that first snap it had just lain, a dead thing which held her without fighting for more. Its tail was fixed in the ground; She had gone in circles, pulling at it, but the tugging fetched more pain up through her tendons, paralyzing her as it latched behind her ears and sent white lights throbbing in her skull.

The skin had parted above the dead teeth. She could see her own meat, with its pale strips of tendon, sheathing the bone.

The thing had no breath, but it smelt like the rusty oil-scummed ditch-pools along the hard trails of Man. You could not bite it – its jaws and its tail were harder than bone.

It was wedged against a salal stem now and she took a first bite at herself. This was how the thing fought – she saw jaws, bared and snapping, in her mind, but they were her own bites reflected back at her. Each bite shocked her into paralysis, she had to fight every command in herself to get back to the wound.

Her muzzle rested against the rusty teeth as she ventured quick, mincing bites. Its smell came over her, inseparable from the taste on her tongue. Through the sweat of pain and fear which was drenching her fur, she could feel the taste of altered things seeping across her skin.

When the bones separated from each other, and the last tendon snapped and curled back into her, She moved off at once. But She did not know what to do. She drank the air which was altered for ever. She found herself going in circles around the place, moving her head right and left, questing for something which was not there anymore. She went down the stream bank, adjusted at once to the stump of her leg working pointlessly under her chin, and sniffed at the traces of Man. There were He and She in the traces, but all blurred and confused. A veil of alterations hung between her and them and the forest. She kept questing in awkward circles.

She retraced her own scent, which was no longer her own, and came back to the stump and the circle she'd dragged in the earth. She sniffed the rusty jaws and tugged loose the mangled fore-leg. She found herself rolling on her back, teasing it between her lips and her other foot. She found she could bite into it now, without the pain coming.

She searched through the litter of leaves and twigs for the strip of fish-flesh which had lured her here last night. She dragged it to the stream, washed off the grit and fibres, and ate it. She was ravenous and thirsty. The water seemed to flow over her thirst – however much she drank she was unsatisfied.

She lay in the shallow water, on the gravel bar, and made gestures of grooming her chest. Rust, oil and other altered things burned at her tongue. She licked at the bead of milk on her first nipple, and remembered.

She went fast, without pausing, but she ran as if she were hiding from herself. She closed her nose and ears to all the messages of the trail, but she was shutting out too the urge to stop and circle every altered thing that she passed.

She went under the trail of Man, through the rusty tunnel, and flattened herself for a moment as a great thing thundered overhead. Then she skirted the ditchpools, flattening her ears in the effort to ignore those messages, and ran beside the piles of sea-logs to the den.

The babies were weak and cold. Two of them managed to whimper to her, only one came crawling out. He butted at her chest with his nose.

She licked his face, nudged him back into the den, and began to groom him, licking the soft fur between the tendons of his neck. He submitted to the grooming, though his face kept pushing at her legs, towards her belly.

She licked again and again, towards the little skull, then turned her head and bit down. The child swerved under her and squealed, but she tightened her grip. The thin blood-jet lingered on her palate for a moment after he was still.

She ate, and then turned to the others, growling and feeding in the close den until there was only left, already dead. She pulled it against her hard, leaking breasts and lay still.

She heard her mate at the entrance. He looked in and signed with his chin but held back, tasting the air and the aura of altered things in the den. She shifted on her side and he came in and sniffed her, giving tiny whistles of greeting as he breathed on the stump of her leg and started to groom the matted fur at her shoulder. But he kept stopping, questing with his nose and mouth round the den.

She sighed and he touched his muzzle to hers, breathing into her nostrils. He licked her face, and then he crouched, and growled.

She reached out to him with her nose, but he crouched lower, fear and confusion in his eyes, the growl coming back in his throat despite himself. She pushed the dead child towards him, and he backed against the den wall. She pushed it closer and bit it on the neck, dragging some flesh away.

The den resounded with his growls, but she pushed the little body against him and stared at his eyes. Still growling, his chin almost to the ground in fear, he looked up at her and bit into the corpse. She watched. His mouth worked upon the meat, but the growls did not stop, and he suddenly leaped away from her, teeth bared, his breath rasping in defiance, before he slunk out.

She sighed again and turned back to the dead child. She licked the exposed meat, and then she turned around and tugged the body against her breasts. She turned again, and could not settle. She needed to drink.

She climbed up on the rocks above the den. The sun was gone, shadows were climbing through the rocks and bushes, the tide was still far down the strand and the sea mumbled with no energy.

Somewhere out on the headland She had drunk once from a rock-pool. It was sea-spray and stale rainwater and She had spat it back, but now it was calling her. It was the drink She must have.

She moved clumsily on the uneven rocks, and at one place missed her footing and slithered into a hollow where coarse grass and thrift sprouted in the sea-shell debris, and a stunted spruce tree grew out of a crevice. Something gasped at her and moved out from the base of the tree. They stared at each other.

The bird was propped on its tattered wings. Its mouth gaped, the pointed tongue was blotched and dry, it gave a tremulous snicker. And gasped.

It has just enough strength to block her way when she moved. It smelled of carrion. The yellow eyes raged, without lustre.

There was an altered thing in it somewhere, she could feel it. The bird had been here for days, it was shedding itself around the tree's base. It had forgotten it was He; it scarcely knew any more that it was Eagle.

She limped towards the best way out but he hopped sideways and almost fell on her. She growled and snapped at his chest, and then dodged as the open beak lunged down at her. One of his wings knocked her down.

Two madnesses faced each other. They stumbled into a dance that was not mating, or killing, and each saw itself in turn reflected in the other's eyes. They hissed as they circled unsteadily, sounds they had never uttered before. The hollow filled with their poisonous breaths.

They could not break free. They came together without intent, as She bit into his belly and he stepped down with all his weight, pinning her with his thumb-talon.

He tasted of dead gull, rotten spent fish. She let go, but he would not. He had no more strength to jab at her, or beat her with his wings; his breath was a shaking drone. All that was left was his will to keep her pinned there.

She went very still, waiting until she sensed that his will was adrift, and then dragged herself out, floundering and pulling even as he came back to life and pressed that clawfoot down. Her skin tore, and she rolled free. He fell back by the tree, eyes staring helplessly at her.

She fled from the rocks, tumbling onto the wet sand. There was a small island in the bay, exposed by the tide, and she made for it, scampering over her own reflection and the glint of the young stars, and the lights of Man, studding the next headland. The brightest star, trembling silver and green in the sea air, sat in the island, on the branch of a dead tree.

Her own breath was the loudest thing in the world, but the shorewind was up and the rain came with it, slanting down from the treeline towards her, eating up the stars.

She fell repeatedly, dragging herself up, sometimes just ploughing forward with her hind legs. By the time she got to the island only one star was left. The rain came down, the tide was running, there were waves breaking already on the island's outer rocks.

She went up through the bushes, past the dead tree, and out on a bare shelf of rock. There was no pool, and no shelter.

The cold began to reach into her. She licked at her chest, and rolled half onto her back, as if she were about to suckle.

The skin of her belly was ripped wide open. She watched, through the membranes, her insides weaving. The rain fell on her, muddied by the sour heat of her bowels and by the milk that oozed out of one torn breast.

She licked at herself and convulsed. She fell back and stared at the last star, almost lost now through the rain and the racing clouds.

Out of her comes a thin, sustained scream.

It goes out into the darkness.

Kapino

HE CAME FROM TAWÁROGHA, where the reef first breaks
as the coastline of Makira dips south into Star Harbour.
When she was sixteen a canoe came down from Bauro on
its way to Santa Anna. There were no blood-debts out-
standing and at that season of the year, with the bonito shoals
about to run, old hatreds could be set aside for trade. The three
strangers stayed the night and looked around and two days later
came back, each on his way home with a new canoe. That afternoon
they joined the frigate bird dance that would call in the bonito to
the reef. In the custom house, lounging beneath the wooden *ayri*
fish which held the ancestors' skulls, they ate betel and storied
until dusk. The youngest, Warihua, turned to the headman's
brother and asked for his daughter in marriage. He paid three
faga, fathom-length strings of red shell money, a good price. At
dawn Warihua left with his bride and his new canoe; the other
chiefs followed soon after. They met up again near Manepuru,
twelve miles past Nauri Bay, and camped for the night. Warihua
deflowered Kapino and handed her over to his friends. Each man
had her again in the morning. She crossed Wainone Bay in the bow
of Warihua's boat, and arrived before dark at her new home,
Suragina.

33

The young chief built a house for her, away from the shore, and she lived there alone. Any man from the village could go to her, and neighbors from Tawani or Pawa, or any stranger on the trail. Warihua made back his investment on Kapino a thousandfold before she got the disease. They say it was leprosy but it may have been yaws, a cousin of syphillis that was the island's curse until the 1950's. They sent her away, across their little peninsula, to a low-lying place that served them as a rubbish-dump. She haunted the spot, sheltering from rain and sun by a huge banyan tree, while her body broke down. When she died the *adaro*, her spirit, moved into the tree. The place was Humou, where Kira Kira stands today.

You might be walking on the trail, or at work in your cutting, or beaching your canoe. Your thoughts are of the girl you desire, or the young wife who waits for you at home. Look up and she is standing there, laughing in your surprise, beckoning. It is as though she has heard your thoughts. And the dream comes true: you make love in the shade of the feather trees and lie together in the close moment of quietening hearts. And the thing in your arms writhes away from you with a harsh cry and a scutter of leaves. A brush turkey, a megapode, flies from your sight into the forest.

You drift home, sick in heart and body. Your strength seems to have left you; you have no energy to work, no appetite. You waste away. Perhaps in a month, perhaps in six, you are gone.

The same for a girl. The young man whose eyes have followed you through the village is suddenly beside you and you give yourself to him as you have secretly dreamed. It is so good, it was meant to be like this. His face, between you and the leafy sky, trembles. And the scrawny bird flies off through the trees, and your spirit fails you.

If you would meet your sweetheart somewhere outside the village, go with her now, or with him. For Kapino will be waiting, with your lover's face, at the appointed hour. Go now, holding your lover's hand. Make no assignations.

When there are many young men in Kira Kira she is often about as a girl. When men are few, she wears a man's skin.

But Kira Kira came after Kapino's time alive, and Suragina has disappeared. The European century waned at the time of her death and twenty years later the High Commission for the British Solomon Islands decreed a presence in Makira Province. The site was chosen and a fine residence built — the only wooden house on the island — for the District Officer. Today the town has swallowed up Bauro and Humou: there are three stores, a hospital, two churches, a cluster of government offices, a soccer pitch. The D.O.'s old residence is now the government rest house where, for $6 a night, a visitor may have a room, a shower and the ministrations of Andrew, the old Santa Cruz houseboy, with his toothless brand of pidgin. And you may have the ghosts too — they walk, they whisper, they knock and on some nights, when lightning flakes the sky across the straits to Ulawa, they rouse the neighborhood dogs to a frenzy and the cocks crow at midnight. Fifty-five years old, the resthouse is crumbling, its plumbing awry; it is a place of dreams and ghosts.

When they built it in 1927 they chose a level place, unused by the natives, fifty yards back from the shore of Humou Bay. Looking out from its huge open common room today, across a clover lawn and through the big acacia trees, you get almost the atmosphere of an English country estate, except for the creepers and orchids that cloak the trees, and the anchorage below with the hills of Arosi in the far west. The first D.O. did not have so fine a view. He found much of his light was excluded by a huge banyan, left by the builders just twenty feet from his front steps. In 1930 he had it cut down.

You can guess the scenario. The new D.O., a bachelor in his twenties, will not see another Englishman till his two-year tour is over. He rises at five to dole out rations and orders for the day. He oversees a small plantation, improvements on the two miles of roadway, recruitments, and the landing of copra. Once a week he sits as magistrate; once a month he tours by canoe around the outlying villages. His day finishes at six. He dresses, correctly, for dinner and is served, alone, course after course at his candlelit table by the houseboy. Afterwards there is more paperwork to do and then an hour with a book, a three-month-old *London Illustrated News*, or a letter for home. To his parents, naturally, and to old school friends or teachers. Each Friday night he writes to his betrothed. Her remote and organdied English charm has nothing whatever in common with the naked Bauro girls who pass murmuring below his window as dusk falls.

The houseboy has gone home; the D.O. is alone in the big house with his letter and his dreams. There is a footfall on the steps — puzzled, he rises and moves to the door: — *"Sally, good lord, it can't be — I must be dreaming." — "No, Phillip, it's true —*

there": and she pinches his wrist, laughing playfully. *"A surprise for you, my dearest. Now don't ask questions and spoil things — I'll explain later..."* Reality flows into the dream he would have scarcely have owned to; joy comes to his bachelor's couch; and the false bird mocks as it flies to the forest behind. *Shame about young Foster, just lost his will to live. One too many bouts of fever, I suppose. Or, you never know, some chaps just aren't cut out for the life — can't cope with the isolation. Now young Stainsby'll make a go of it — was three years below me at Charterhouse — self-reliant sort of cove, level-headed as they come....*

Well, no. Perhaps, as they used to say in Arosi, the English soul is in pawn to a devil more potent than any tropical goblin. Kapino did not seduce that D.O., or any other. She turned on taps, prowled in the night, hurled crockery round the kitchen, and threw ping pong balls at him during dinner.

Ping pong balls.

That's why I spoke of ghosts. I can't believe in Kapino's spirit sporting with brass tops or celluloid toys. The D.O. taped up his doors and shuttered his windows, and still the balls came pocking across the mahogany floor, the water ran, the cups and saucers sailed in the night. There's no doubt about that ghost — it was a constant menace to D.O.'s and their visitors, missionaries included. Eventually they built a smaller residence nearer the shore, tore out some inner walls in the old building and turned it into a resthouse. The town was growing by now: there was a police detachment, many more visitors and eventually as many as three D.O.'s at a time.

The hauntings continued. One night two English police officers came pounding on the new residence door in the early hours. The ghost had driven them out. Old Andrew, who was houseboy to several D.O.'s and has tended the resthouse for nearly thirty years, told me about the ghost with a rich pantomime of flashing palms, starting eyes, shuddering lips and moans that was as much his natural style as an attempt to compensate for our limited verbal understanding. But, except that the poltering affected only single or unaccompanied men, there seems little in common between these malicious pranks and the devil woman's vendetta. For that continues too. In the last few years two native men have followed the phantom into the dusk and have wasted away, beyond the doctors' help or diagnoses.

Yet everyone in Kira Kira identifies the poltergeist with the devil woman. The resthouse's register contains a running commentary by visitors on her behavior or her non-appearance. Many entries are ribald or scoffing yet the bedroom doors are carefully locked at night. Why a turned key should deter a succubus when it couldn't even stop a ping pong ball, I cannot guess.

For me the strangest thing about the resthouse was the way the walls shifted and swam whenever I looked around. It was like those near-estatic moments of blind vertigo that you get in adolescence when you stand up suddenly, and it wasn't too hard to account for. On my first stay there I'd still been adjusting to the heat and humidity of the Solomons, and when I'd passed through again I was eating great quantities of betel. This time I had just got off the government steamer *Betua* after beating up the coast all day from Star Harbor with one engine shot and a high sea running in Wainone Bay. The earth seemed unmoored: like Falesa it "heaved like s ship's deck." I was on my way home and this time, instead of twenty-four hours, I had two days and two nights to relax in Kira Kira before I left for Guadalcanal.

I climbed the resthouse steps as dusk came in. Andrew greeted me with a great show of delight, crowing like a rooster and crossing the common room floor with his palm upraised to grab mine. I'd never seen him quite so animated. My friend Marua, the Gilbertese postmaster who has a permanent room in the house, was pouring beer into the old man: "Andrew's a grandfather again." One of his daughters is married to a Makira man and her first-born, a girl, had come into the world the night before. I toasted her in Foster's Lager — "Wanem now name blong dis pickanin?" Andrew shrugged and giggled — "No savvy dis time. See byembye." He mimed his daughter with the child at her breast, and the proud father strutting. Around the couple's home, next to Andrew's out behind the washhouse, a crowd of visitors sat talking softly, eating betel, smoking in the shadows.

The three of us planned a big meal for the next night, my last in Makira. Andrew had yam, *pana, ruruta, kumara* and slippery cabbage and I went and bought meat the next morning. Then I walked across the peninsula, down through Tawani and Pawa and six more miles along the trail to Ravo River. I was absorbing all I could on this last day, getting details into my notebook that my memory might filter out, concentrating on textures of sound and smell. I swam for a while in the Ravo — visually identical to rivers like the Thompson, atmospherically completely other — and headed back through the afternoon. We were to eat at seven and I was back at the resthouse in good time for a shower and change. The last of the sun across the bay threw my shadow up the steps and over the common room floor; the house was full of the smell of cooking; but Andrew had lost his gaiety. He huddled in an old jacket, hugging his shoulders and shivering. Marua said "Andrew not feel so god — old people feel change in weather more than us." I couldn't detect any temperature drop at all. Andrew served the feast and disappeared — the conversation flagged. — "Ne'mind" said Marua, "old man Andrew got no teeth — can't eat the meat anyway," but it was depressing to hear the gaunt houseboy shifting from chair to chair in the common room, grumbling to himself. We sent him home and I decided to go to bed. I had to be up at five anyhow: there was a market tomorrow and I wanted to send a sack of betel nuts down to my friends in Ghupuna. We said goodnight.

There was a firefly in my room and I closed the door without turning the light on. Down in Star Harbour they believe the winking green lamps are the spirits of the dead and I'd never been able to look at one closely. Of course they laugh now at the old superstition, but if a firefly comes indoors in the evening no one relaxes until it has been chased back out. This one was not, in fact, inside: I found it was clinging to the mosquito-mesh window, its light pulsing slowly, turning about as if trying to worm its way in. Outside, other lampyres were drifting singly across the night, under the still acacia boughs and down towards the shore. I leant my head against the mesh to watch my visitor, and found the larval reality behind the faery gleam. Its maggot-like belly, mealy colored and slack, was exposed and repulsive. I preferred the look of it from across the room, and watched it for awhile as I undressed, pulled my laplap over me and lay down.

Sleep didn't come. Maybe I'd gone to bed too early; perhaps my mind was unwilling to let go of a place I'd be leaving tomorrow for years, possibly for ever. Could be I was upset about Andrew's sickness and the gloomy dinner. In any case, few writers bother to analyse their insomnia — it exists and the only antidote is to exploit it. I got up, turned on the light and unpacked my larger notebook. There were a dozen things I could work on — three new story ideas and one half-writtem, and several passages for the novel which had brought me to the Solomons in the first place. I didn't want to try anything too immediate, undistilled, and I turned to a section I'd left unfinished back home. It was about a child dying: a baby who just stared like an old man into people's faces, wouldn't suckle, and yawned all the time. The image had come from a book I'd read long ago about the Scottish island, St. Kilda. It had haunted me for years and now I was trying to make it my own. It was right for the novel. But I wasn't working well — part of my writing pattern is sanity-breaks for coffee, and though I did once put on my laplap and open the door I hesitated to go to the kitchen. I didn't want to disturb anyone in the house and one visiting couple had a fractious child who might well wake, and stay awake. Besides, they might have mistaken my footfalls for the ghost's!

So I wrote and savagely erased, for another hour. There was some vital thing missing. I couldn't capture those dark eyes in the little alien face staring through its incomprehensible brief visit. I smoked and tried again, and leaned my head on my hands. There was a footstep on the coral path outside. Then silence. I turned back to my much-scored page and heard the noise again. A single crunch, like a foot upon gravel, as if a waiting man had shifted his feet or was poised to move again. In the rural Solomon's, most of all in Makira, one has no fears for property or life but it seemed unnatural, all the same, for a native to be out alone at that hour, apparently loitering by the resthouse steps. I sat very still and heard it again — a soft double footstep on the crushed coral. And silence. I didn't like it. I went and turned off the light and, after a moment, moved stealthily to the big mesh window. There was nothing: someone had even left a light on in the common room and it spilled down the front steps onto the white path. Beyond, across the grass, the big trees were completely still. A few fireflies, the light wash of the anchorage, nothing else. I heard the sound again — a footstep and the scrape of the other foot drawing towards it. There was nothing on the path. For a moment it seemed a grass clump twitched at the light's edge. I thought a dog, but there was none.

Anyone who has experienced the supernatural knows that its hallmark is certainty. You don't *wonder* in the presence of spirits. But I hardly entertained the possibility. Maybe sound carried strangely at night; maybe a mole or a creeping shrew threw a magnified sound in the stillness. I wasn't rationalizing — I knew there was an explanation and was uneasy at not guessing it. Eventually I went and lay down and still, intermittently, that presence moved outside. I lay tense in the darkness, longing for sleep, shuffling words that had slipped from their moorings, gleaning scraps of conversation from a nonexistent room through the outside wall.

A rooster screamed and jerked me back from my half-sleep. It cried again, full-throated, from behind the house and was challenged instantly by another and another. Every rooster from Humou to Bauro was at once aroused and screaming down the darkness. A rooster's speech is shaped in the listener's ear — to the French it's *coc-a-rico* and in England, of course, *cock-a-doodle-doo*, but who has ever heard that call three-syllabled? Those roosters called, repeatedly, three notes; and KAP-EE-NOHH, KAP-EE-NOHH was their burden to my infected ear.

Then the dogs started up. From every quarter, straining the leashes of distance, hurling volleys of rage and possession through the night. The roosters were almost drowned out by the barking, and I could hear the scamper on coral and grass become a gallop as the dogs packed up and chased their own cries around the houses. It seemed incredible that anyone in Kira Kira could stay asleep through this — perhaps, like me, they were all lying unnerved and silent in their beds. There was madness in the clamor, like the void in a peacock's scream, but there was power too. It seemed that a hunt was afoot, and one group of dogs came baying under the high resthouse floor, emerged from beneath my room and tore off again towards an answering pack by the wash-house. In that instant, at a stroke, the pandemonium ceased. There was total silence for perhaps six heartbeats and then, through its fullness, the sound of a woman. Wailing.

This time the flesh did shrink against my skin, and the hairs of my neck went crawling. I knew this was something unearthly: a cry from an abandoned soul, a terrible lament. *Eah, eah, eah, eah* came her voice, the one focus of the night, rising and falling in a desolate, repeated cadence. To be alone and to be abandoned are not the same thing. I was alone and content to be so, but that wretched outcast creature in the night was crying out of a loss so total that I was appalled beyond fear. My western mind could only cope by humanizing, and "*Alas poor ghost*" I whispered like a prayer, as though my small compassion could bring anything to the abused spirit who saw sweet life and love receding from her. In a pagan world where there is no self, she was forced back upon herself and *eah, eah, eah, eah,* the grief of that emptiness wailed through the night again and again.

There was no let up. Her voice was very close to the house, a little softer now, and, strangely, I was falling asleep. Briefly I wondered if my surge of pity was a response to the most seductive siren song of all, but I was slipping away and the next thing my door was pounding and Marua was booming — "Shona, market!"

Out in the common room old Andrew was standing by the steps, staring out at the bay. — "Hey, *mela,*" I said, "you orrait nomore?" He shook his head curtly, almost rude, and turned slightly away without looking at me. At the bathroom door Marua was just coming from his shower. I gestured towards the old man — "Andrew's still feeling crook." Marua shook his head — "No, he's better now" he said "Just that little girl died in the night."

Maria

I cry. I am the crying she hears, the child weeping
inside her dream. I am crying and will not stop.
She struggles to escape into the light. My tears
are embedded in her own moaning. She is desperate
to come awake.

She knows me. She has heard me before. She must have
dreamed of this before I came to her. But I have never
been so close. Now she contains the crying that overwhelms
her. I'll be with her still, when she wakes.

I am only a cry, a child's cry of fear and foreboding
inside her. I came as a cry, stretched and fearful
across the grey city. I cried myself into her
dream, she accommodates me.

I am greedy and I suffer inside her suffering, sucking
upon her blood and her memory. I will survive.

She gasps as if there were not enough air for both
of us. I am at home in her. We must learn each other's
names before we can become strangers.

I am crying. Her fear overwhelms me.

RENÉ'S EYES OPEN as Terry struggles beside him. She has
dragged the top sheet into a rope away from him. There's
just enough light from the window for him to see her,
thrashing upon the pillow as though she were drowning.
The fingers of one hand scrabble before her mouth like someone
dying, and terrible sounds are coming out of her.

As he reaches over, the turmoil crescendoes, her moans are threaded by a thin whimpering, her hand clutches the sheet and she sits up: she is rigid and staring, it ends with a convulsive gasp.

"What is it?" he says. "What were you dreaming?"

Her head snaps round, she stares at his face, like a child in fever. Her mouth is open, her green eyes blank in their white surrounds. He strokes her shoulder; the skin is clammy.

And she flinches from his touch, pulling the sheet against her and backing away across the bed. "Easy", he says. "Easy. Soi tranquille, hein? It was just one of your dreams." Her eyes are in focus now, but he could still be a stranger. Her head drops sullenly, she mutters to her knees: "I always have bad dreams when you stay over." He shrugs and lies back. A blackbird starts in, outside the window. His eyes move from her face to the draped sheet – her skin there, flowing from her ribs, to her hip, to her thigh. He reaches across again.

She swings her legs off the bed: "I'll go sleep on the couch."

"It's your bed," he says, "that's crazy. I'll go."

But she's moving already, past the end of the bed towards the door. He watches the set of her shoulders, the line of her calves. He pulls the quilt over him and turns back, sighing, on his pillow. Birds are singing everywhere down the street.

At 9:30 he calls from the doorway: "You better get up. I made coffee."

She turns onto her back and smiles, sleepily. Her hand reaches out from the sheet: "Come here. Lie with me a minute." "There's not much time," he says, but he goes over. He sits on the couch and holds her hand, but his mind's already at the office. Her eyes seek his, her smile ingratiates: "I hate those shitty dreams. I'm sorry." She pulls the back of his hand up to her cheek. "I'm sorry. There's this one I keep having – I just can't get out of it."

Talking about it has brought tears up in her eyes. "Okay," he says, "but now you have to get up."

"Can I see you tonight?"

He laughs, short but pleased: "I imagine so, poupée. Why not?" She lets him kiss her at the crown of her head.

He stands up. She takes a breath and lifts her chin as though to speak, but thinks better of it. Rises instead with her usual abruptness and heads for the bathroom. She brushes past him – his hands reach for her instinctively. "I know," she says from across the hall. "I'm so young and beautiful, and I'm a pain in the ass too. You needn't say it!" He shrugs.

The hot water hisses between her shoulder blades and around her ears. She exales loudly – *Aaagh* and again, *Aaagh*, a delighted shudder passing through her legs, body, arms. She is warm all through – she turns her face into the shower's jet. The night's uneasy echoes recede, she blows into the waterfall, *Wubble-bubble*, like a child, and breathes in deeply before she snaps the lever down. The water tumbles round her ankles now. She swills a washcloth around the bath with her foot and lets the tap run on, for it is when she bends down that the nausea comes – uncoiling from the pit of her stomach up through her throat to her face – and she delays as long as she can.

But there's nothing; she is almost reluctant to believe it. She steps from the bath and moves with a kind of elation to the washbasin, and the mirror.

> There is the face that will be mine while I'm with her. It is almost familiar. The eyes and the nostrils that will let the world into me. She leans towards her reflection. What is new in her eyes? I stare back through her.
>
> Her flesh is sweet and strong about me. I reach out for the limits of her skin. She is brave and beautiful. We will survive.
>
> Her fingers press softly upon the mouths of her breasts.
>
> She is singing for me.

She hears the doorbell through the water's chute in the toilet. She goes to the window, stands on tiptoe and wipes her palm through the steam on the upper pane.

Her father's car is down by the curb. Someone's looking out at the rear window. A boy? Dark face. There are voices in the kitchen.

"Shit!" She has nothing to cover herself.

She wraps the wet towel around her and goes out.

In the moment before they see her, they are two middle-aged men framed by a doorway. A snapshot of awkwardness. René has less hair than her father.

Daddy's eyes bolt from her semi-nudity. His meek hand gestures to René. Daddy's clothes and hands conspire against himself – his weakness and humility enrage her.

René starts to speak for him: "Your father says –"

"What do you want? Why did you come here?"

Her father ducks his head, his eyes come up beseechingly, wavering at her bare thighs. "I'm sorry, Terry."

"Well?". She hears, and hates, her mother in herself.

"Your Mother's in the hospital, Terry," and his eyes fall away again. "I believe she is dying... She asked to see you."

She moves towards him: "Oh Dad, I'm sorry. You could have phoned – you should be there –"

His cringing is dreadful. His eyes yearn to accept her pity, but: "Your *real* mother, Terry."

Her snake eyes remind him just how much she is not his.

"René – find me a cigarette. I'm getting dressed."

She's still tugging her jeans closed when she returns: "How did she know where to find you?"

"She's always known. What could I do, Terry? – her husband sent their son round to the house. I had to come for you..."

"She's always known?"

"We agreed she shouldn't interfere with your life."

"You never told me you knew her."

"We agreed. She understood. Mummy thought it was best for you –"

Terry dunks her cigarette in the cold coffee. Maybe she is going to be sick today after all.

It passes. "I'm ready."

He gets up the courage to say, "Do you think you should dress like that for the hospital?"

"Yes," she says. And sees from the door that her father is taking in the kitchen he's never seen: the ketchup spill down the stove front, the dishes by the sink, the Pizza Hut box on the floor up against the Safeway bag, angular with garbage.

Not his own cozy little hell.

René takes her arm. She kisses him brusquely. He'd like to have played it domestic. "Don't come to work, Terry," he says, "but call me if you want. I'll come around about seven. Don't get upset, hein?" They are public utterances. "Au revoir, Mr. Dawson – good to 'ave met you at last" as he closes the door. René's face can be tough, and ugly.

The car smells exactly as it did when they bought it. Clean, factory vinyl. Blister-pack seat covers. The boy huddles against the back door. "Hi," she says and reaches to pull the ashtray out. It's never been used. Her father adjusts his seatbelt, the Rotarian badge on his key-ring trembles as the engine starts up. He depresses the handbrake: "This is Tony," he says.

"Hi," she says again.

Her husband sent their son round to the house – jesus: "You're my brother."

He stares back. The car moves out from the curb. Her chin is on the seat-back, she searches for herself in him: what does *he* see?

> There are openings in her skin.
> He is almost familiar.
> A dream inside a dream. He is searching too.
> Come in. Come in.
> He is brave.

"Are there any others?" she says. "You got any brothers, sisters?"

He mumbles something. He looks down.

"What?"

"Gracey and Alice." It's like a whisper, his lips scarcely move. He makes her feel strident.

"How old are they?"

He squints at his hands: "Seven, I guess. Alice was just five last week."

She smiles. His lips mirror politely. "I always wanted a sister," she says. "I never thought of a brother." He shrugs – she lunges down and catches his wrist: "So, do I look like Her? How sick is She?"

He doesn't understand why he trusts her.

"She went asleep last evening." His bottom lip leads, accenting his murmuring voice: "She ain't going to wake up. Never."

He would like to tug his hand free, but he daren't. His eyes check her father. "You must be sad," she says. "I'm sorry."

They pass the plastic buffalo by the exhibition grounds. Then the brown spike of the bible college. He stares out at them.

She releases his wrist, turns to her father: "Tell me about her."

Daddy's rimless glasses, his pale hands at ten-to-two on the wheel, the sparse hairs on his knuckles, riddle her with irritation.

He looks sideways for a moment, clears his throat, lifts his head to concentrate on the traffic. The message is *The boy's listening, Mummy could be listening, don't make things difficult...*

She whirls back again to her brother. He's backed up against the upholstery, his dirty fingernails press into the denim on his knees, the Indian face avoids hers. "I didn't know," she says. "That she was a native, I mean. That I am. I used to wonder –"

"My Dad's Metis," he says.

He's a nice looking kid. "How old are you?"

"Eleven years."

"I'm ninteen."

"I know." There's the ghost of a real smile, but not for her.

The car pulls over. "I won't go into the parking lot, Terry," her father rolls down his window. "I'll wait for you here."

The boy watches for her lead. "Okay," she says, and yanks at the door handle. "C'mon, Tony – you better show me the way."

Crossing the street, she almost reaches for his hand. He walks stolidly beside her. Halfway through the lot he points across her: "That's my Dad's truck." A white pickup, with a fuel tank in back. "What's his name, your Dad?" "Jim Coulter." "I thought Metis had French names." They start up the wide steps below the *Admissions* sign, and a dread she hasn't felt since school fumbles under her heart. Tony pulls at the big glass door: "His grandfather was Scotch. Hudson Bay Man."

She hesitates, squinting back into the sun-glare of the cars and the concrete. "Jesus, I hate hospitals," she says. "Me too" – he startles her by spitting down onto the step behind them. The spermy dreg winks from the hot cement.

It's all like TV except for the smell. Even the corridor-sounds have the tinny remoteness of TV. Hospitals, retirement homes, prisons, schools – the quarantined communities that you never need remember. Sick flesh, old flesh, hopeless bodies with insane, important eyes. She finds that her fists are clenched, that she's walking beside her brother without drawing breath. She breathes out with a long, shuddering effort. A burst of laughter comes from a nurses' lounge to their left.

There's a man with a floor polisher, two oriental nurses carrying blankets, two sag-mouthed wheelchair-cases parked in front of a TV set, one of them sleeping. Nightmares within nightmares.

Tony moves ahead, then stops at the door of a small ward. Room for three beds. He stares at the empty one under the window. Outside, two cottonwoods and beyond them the pitch of the Roughriders' stand. A nurse steps past Terry: "She's gone, Tony – I'm sorry." She's black, wavy-haired, her smile's unfeigned; she puts her arm round the boy's shoulders. He stares at the bed – it's made up, waiting. And to Terry: "You her sister? You've got the same mouth."

Terry shakes her head. Why can't she say it? "Tony's my brother."

Then: "Can I see her?"

"Surely," the nurse says. "I wouldn't suggest you take Tony, though."

"Where's my Dad?" he asks, eyes still on the bed.

"He's down at the office, honey. I'll take you along for a coke just now – he has a few papers to sign."

And left, down the corridor: "You'd never think she had a girl your age."

Terry wants to hug the poor kid. She needs to. But the nurse is between them, her arm around him still; he accepts that easily. He hasn't looked at *her* once.

And doesn't when the nurse knocks on a green door, unlocks it herself, and holds it open. Her smile is gentle: "We'll be down at Reception. Okay?"

There's an alcove with a desk and a filing cabinet by a frosted window. A man in green fatigues, writing; there's a rubber glove on his left hand. The door closes of itself. He looks up: "Hello?"

Terry reaches for the name: "Coulter," she says. "My mother?"

He looks her over curiously. "You don't need to, you know." He strips off the glove. "Your father's signed all the papers."

"I want to."

He nods to the table beside her. She hadn't noticed. It's on castors; there's a huge double sink beyond it.

Not like TV – there doesn't seem room for a body inside the blanket's contours.

"Want me to do it?"

She shakes her head, her back's towards him already. She senses his tactful retreat to the alcove.

> I have shut myself up in her.
> There are cold winds around her.
> The grey city.

Her skin closes against them.
I shall sleep. I can trust her. We move closer together.

If there were a pillow under the head it would seem less unreal.
There's nothing there, she's come too late, she knows this at once.
The top lip falls strangely, pointed, upon the lower. Nostrils
pinched. There's a hint of white under one of the eyelids. René says
thát her eyes roll up when she's coming.

Yes, it's a young face, young shoulders. But it's empty, casual as
a cat's carcass by a ditch. The hair could be living – black like her
own, but thicker, it shines a little under the strip lights. It must
have been long – it disappears under the shoulders. Terry touches
it, hooks a finger through it. The cheekbone is cold, unexpected;
but then the room, she realises, is cold.

"What did she die of?" She turns and leans her bum on the table.
The man looks over, file in hand. His eyes move from her thighs to
the dead face beside her. "You don't know?"

"It's the first time I've seen her." Something about that makes
sense to him.

"Pneumonia," he says. He put the file down and comes over. How
could he look at his wife's body, at his kids, after a day's work here?
But his eyes aren't cold, not even indifferent. He reaches for the
blanket – she gestures to stop him. "She only had one lung, you see
– T.B.: they're pretty susceptible to it."

His pale eyes ask permission. He covers the face. Just a strand of
hair lies exposed.

"I guess she wasn't too strong. And farming's a hard life. Young
kids, too – shouldn't have had them really. The last one was a
caesarean."

"But she looks so young."

"Thirty one, if you can trust the records. Yes. Guess she was just
a kid when she had you?"

"I guess so."

"Adopted out, were you?"

She nods.

"Ah, well," he says. "We have to make the best of what life
provides us, eh?"

Terry shakes her head, incredulous at what neither she nor the
man understand. "I should go," she says. "Thanks."

"You take care now." He holds the door open for her.

She nods again. Takes a wrong turning, walks back past the green door. She could do with a beer.

She's going to tell her father to go on home; she'll walk. She stops outside the doors to light a cigarette. Finds herself looking for Tony's spittle on the step. The sun has eaten it.

I am quick. I whisper through her cells.

She is free, and breathing for me again, and I recognise what she does not know.

I unfurl in her, we are alone and sufficient, I blossom behind her eyes.

Ah, yes.

Life reaches towards me, I am drawn out of myself.

Her eyes are drawn through the parking lot, across the glancing light and the hot shadows. The man's face turns at the same time. He drops his forearm from the pickup roof. The young face at the window beside him, the white pickup.

Each takes an uncertain step but then, as she moves cautiously down towards the ambulance bay, he heads across. It seems to her that he controls the space between them, so that even as his body turns and sidesteps to thread the ranks of cars his eyes are fixed on her and his feet never deviate. Cowboy heels, and jeans that fit snug over his boots. He treads lightly for a big man, he commands his body.

He looks up from the foot of the steps. "You're Teresa," he says. A tremor through her that those arms could break her in half, but would never choose to. She goes down till her face is level with his. The eyes look into her: native-brown but not passive or opaque. She sees no pain.

He extends his hand. Farm hands of birth and death, hard but not brutalised. She stands there, she senses the hand reaching to touch her body.

You dumb bitch, she tells herself, there's just been too much going on all at once, you're flipping out. She takes the hand: "Terry," she says.

He nods. "Jim Coulter."

Between them the man-woman appraisal. Body and mind in the

sunlight. He nods again. She says, "I'm sorry," and looks down, shrugging, lets go his hand, reaches in her purse for another smoke. He watches.

"I don't know what to say." She blows smoke from the side of her mouth, away from his face, sees Tony watching from the pickup. "I mean, I want to ask you all kinds of stuff. But, like, I'm intruding right now, right?"

His eyes fix between her breasts. He folds his arms: "Ask what you want," he says. "She wanted you here."

He must have learned long ago not to be awkward with himself. He stands there, waiting, concentrated, ignoring the cars that swing close by them, the straggle of people up and down the steps.

"Christ, I don't even know her name," she says. "I meant to ask Tony."

His chin flicks up, there's a hint of defiance: "Her name was Maria. We called her Marie. Marie Metcalfe." It's final as a tombstone. He's slipping back into himself – that first spark of approval gone.

"Well, was it sudden? I mean –"

"She's been dying for two years." The words are careful, the voice curiously educated. Still no pain there. He looks at her flatly: "She was never well, since I knew her."

"How old was she then? When was that?"

"Come over to the truck," he says. "I don't wish to leave Tony alone." She follows at once. He looks ahead as he speaks: "She came to me when Tony was four."

"He's not her son, then?"

"Yes, he came with her."

"So he's not yours."

"He has my name."

He carries his hardness so easily. He robs her of her own poise. She moves quickly, to keep up with him, wishes he'd notice her. He stops as a car backs out in front of them. "Who'll look after him?" she demands. "And the girls – Gracie, isn't it, and –"

"They stay with their Auntie," he says, impatient, and steps round the fender of a panel-van. She has to hurry again.

"My mother's sister?"

He turns back – it must be contempt on his face: "My sister. Marie had no family."

She's only half following the words. She wants to play this *right* in his eyes. His jaw-tilt again: "We didn't talk about her family. She saw her mother in the city sometimes, I didn't meet her. Maria didn't go to the funeral. She had no time for her father."

They're beside the pickup. Tony's eyes are fixed on his father's face.

"Where were they from, Jim?" there's a weakness in using his name. He doesn't accept it: "Hartley," he says. "He ran the store." And, as he heads round to the driver's side: "I wouldn't go up — there's nothing there for you."

"What about your place? Nothing for me there either?"

He turns and places one hand on the hood ornament, a leaping silver ram: "You should just leave things be," he says. "Get on with your life, Terry."

His eyes take in her neckline and trace the side of her face. They linger on her hair. Tony's face, just two feet away, is averted.

"Couldn't I come out sometime — see Tony and the girls? I mean, they *are* my sisters."

"I don't see what that would achieve." He moves again and opens the pickup door. "Look after yourself, Terry."

"Well, fuck you too," she says, quiet and venemous,and turns on her heel. Then thinks, in mid-stride, she should speak to Tony.

Coulter hasn't moved. "I appologise," he says, and loses no strength in saying it. "Her funeral is on Saturday. Two o'clock in Lebret. You will be welcome."

She does not move till they've driven off. Coulter touches his hat. She winks at Tony; his hand lifts in a tiny wave.

> I have to learn what she has to learn.
> She has to learn what I know.
>
> Her shadow overtakes mine in this empty place.
>
> We cast the same shadow under the sun-wheel.

Terry lights another cigarette. The sun is merciless. She's going to stop in at the Horseshoe Tavern and look at some natives, eavesdrop. Jesus, she thinks, jesus, son of a bitch, this is unreal.

And by the time she reaches the car she has changed her mind again.

Daddy is making tidy annotations in his CAA book. She gets in beside him: "I guess you wouldn't lend me the car for the weekend, would you?"

"What do you want it for?"

"Just yes or no, Daddy, alright?" She takes the CAA book, and leafs through the map-pages.

"I couldn't do that, Terry. There's the shopping to do tomorrow, and Church on Sunday morning –"

"You could use a cab, couldn't you?" But she's given up. She finds Hartley in the index, turns to the page.

"Be reasonable," he says. "Besides, Mummy might like to go for a drive."

Terry butts out her cigarette in the ashtray. It's been cleaned out already. "Well I want to go to my Mother's funeral," she says.

"I'm sorry," he says. "Oh, dear."

"Skip it," she says. Hartley's not far from Lupton, she was through there once. "I just want to get away for a few days, that's all."

"Same old Terry," he smiles, but unhappily. "Always, out of the blue, some impractical impulse. Mummy used to worry, you know, that you might be a little – unbalanced."

"Oh, jesus."

"I always took your side on that point, Terry."

Daddy's face always came round doorways like a turtle's, expecting the worst. "Were you worried I'd turn out like her?" Terry slaps the book shut.

"We didn't know her, Terry. We only heard from her once."

"When was that?"

He sighs, nervously starts the engine. "She sent something, when you were seven."

"What?"

"A card," he says, "and a little dress. It was absurd really – frilly, nylon, hideous. And far too small for you."

"But you didn't give them to me."

His face wants to run and hide. He drives carefully out into the traffic, and stops at the next intersection, on an orange light.

"You could have got through before it changed."

"Oh, Terry."

"So what color was it? The dress."

"I don't remember, Terry – white I suppose –"

"And what did you do with it?"

"It was so long ago. I imagine it went to the Salvation Army." And, as he drives off again, before she can start in, "We wrote your mother and told her it would be best for everyone if she didn't contact you. It's not as if she'd shown any interest for the first six years of your life." He only ever spoke forcefully when he was quoting Mummy.

"She may have changed or – seen things differently."

"Mummy and I had to think of you."

"This'll do", she says, as they cross 12th Avenue, "right here" and has the door open before he's stopped. She gives him the hug that she thinks was meant for Tony and he murmurs in embarrassment.

"Bye," she says, and runs back and across the street as the lights change.

The meridan trees arch over 12th, it's the prettiest vista in the city, in summer, but the houses are faded after the first two blocks, some derelict and slumping, waiting for apartment developers or for the middle-class to redeem them. The only garden intact for the last block is at the De-Tox house. A group of men lounge on the stoop there, a native youth, about her age, adjusts the lawn sprinkler. She's been noticing pregnant women, now she's noticing natives. She remembers Daddy rolling on the lawn with her, under the sprinkler jets. She strides across the parking lot, patting René's grey Saab as she passes.

Carla's at the desk: "Hi, René told me. How is she?"

"She was gone," Terry says. "Hell, I'd never met her – forget it... René busy?"

"I'll call him," Carla turns to the console. "No, it's only some voice-over shit – go on through."

In the viewing room a crumpled actor with a young voice talks into a mike as he watches the screen. Underwater shots of coral, then a boat full of beautiful people off a beach. A girl surfaces in a snorkel mask.

"You hear your own breathing, and the beat of your flippers, and at the same time you can listen to the cicadas and the parrots in the palms on the shore just above you. You are between worlds. And beneath you stretches the paradise garden of the reef, ablaze with its living jewels, the fish..."

"We'll try it," a woman calls. Ann Friessen. "Thanks, David." The lights come up. "What d'you think, René?"

"It's okay," he stands up at the front, waves at Terry. "But for me, it would work better in a girl's voice..."

"Like 'Come on in' instead of 'This is the score'?"

"Yes, I guess so."

"Okay, we'll try that." Ann waves to Terry too. "Who've we got?"

"I do a marvellous Gidget," the actor pipes, falsetto. Everyone laughs.

René comes up to the door. "You alright, poupée? I said not to come in?"

"She was dead already. No big deal." They walk out to his office.

Terry takes a cigarette from the box on his desk. "She was native, René. Imagine that. I'm half-indian."

"Not so much of a surprise, hein?"

"No. I used to wonder ... Doesn't bother you?"

He throws up his hands and leans on the desk beside her. Some of his mannerisms remind her of how much older he is, and how foreign.

"Eh, be real, kid. There's no old family in Québec without some Indian blood – what's the difference?"

Terry draws patterns in the ashtray with her match-stub. "So if you knocked me up and I had a brown baby –"

"Hiawatha Lauzon. Sounds great." Carla is at the door with a stack of magazines.

René gets up and twirls, turning the moment into a skit. "You are never boring, ma poupeé," he says, waltzing round the desk. "You could for sure make trouble for the wrong man."

"Sorry," Terry says. "I never said it."

Carla winks at René and dumps the magazines on the coffee table. It's never occurred to Terry that Carla has been there too.

"No problem," René laughs, "But now I have to announce to my colleagues that I have a vasectomy!"

"Vasectomies don't always take."

He leans back in his chair: "This one will!"

Carla raps twice on the wooden desk top and heads for the door. "Pray for rain," she says.

"Well?" says René.

"Can you lend me a car."

He checks her eyes: "You going somewhere?"

"I want to go to her funeral. She had a sexy husband."

"Oh, yes? When is it?"

"Saturday."

"So why don't I take you? You could feel out of place, or –"

"No, I want to get off anyway, think about some stuff. Can you lend me a car?"

"Sure," he shrugs. "You can have the Saab."

"You won't need it?"

"Not if you're out of town!"

Won't your wife wonder? What'll you –"

"I told you. How many times must I tell you? At my age you don't waste time with small lies. No problem, okay?"

"Okay, great. Where's the keys?"

"You don't mess about, kid!" She still can't resist the fine lines at his eyes. She wants to lean over and run her hands inside his shirt, but she's in high gear. "Come on... please."

He digs out his key-ring, and separates a smaller ring with two keys and the *Capricorn* medallion on it.

"Thanks." She mimes a kiss to him, grabs an Ovation mint from the bowl on the coffee table and goes out with it wedged in her lips like a cheroot. "Bye!" she calls.

"Drive carefully, poupée."

She walks past the empty front desk, tossing the keys up and catching them like the girl in his Jeep commercial.

She leaves the car running outside the apartment, stuffs a bag with a few days' things, takes all the beers from the fridge and puts them back in the carton, and runs out.

She takes the Lewvan to the ring road, swings north and then boots it to the highway.

She didn't even tell him where she was going. He didn't even ask.

What will he say when he knows that his child is growing inside her? If she tells him.

The fields of flax and canola are a chequerboard of mauve and yellow, wheeling away on both sides. Almost mesmeric. Now Rape is called Canola; now undertakers are Funeral Directors.

She gulps at her beer and lodges the bottle between her thighs. The car is so quiet and luxurious. She plays with the air-conditioning, the windows, the mirrors, the seat-adjustments – all the electronic buttons. This must be what slumming is like, she thinks, for the very rich.

She presses the tape which projects from the cassette deck. Keith Jarrett. Well, what the hell...

> She takes me to be with herself.
> Inside her, inside this moving room, across the wide
> land.
>
> The sun wheels, the fields peel back,
> I see through her eyes.
>
> We pursue each other.

She rummages·in the pile of cassettes on the seat beside her. "Wish You Were Here," "Pat Garrett and Billy The Kid," Joan Armatrading, Van Morrison. She's looking for highway music. There's a kid's drawing mixed up with the cassettes – a man, a woman, a dog, a house, a spider-sun; green, yellow, red, and I LOVE YOU DAD, JE T'AIME PAPA filling most of the page.

What a rat's nest. She doesn't want to deal with that shit. She isn't over this morning yet, too much stuff going down all at once, and that shitty dream again, the terrified child, still lingering, doomy. Where the hell does it come from? – she can't be sure if she's always had it or if it's just the vague dread she used to wake up to, taking the form of a crying child. Maybe it goes with pregnancy, like the sickness that didn't come this morning.

She comes over the hill past the monastery, down towards Craven and the valley's edge. Hardly a vehicle on the glaring blacktop. She ejects the piano tape, picks out "Court and Spark" and slips it in, pressing *fast forward* and band *3* on the display.

It's a wonder to her that René hasn't noticed the change in her boobs. She can't work out if the child crying in her dream is really young, or maybe 12 or 13, scared back into little-girlhood. Maybe it's something she's forgotten from her own childhood, a playback.

The stereo clicks, the green *play* light pulses. Okay.

She presses the button to tilt back her seat and then, as the song starts:

> "*He was drinking in the lounge of the Empire Hotel*
> *He was drinking for diversion*
> *He was thinking of himself*

she adjusts the speaker buttons and the volume so the tune jumps into life behind her. She floors the pedal, lifts her chin, and sings out. She's flying...

> *Drinking alone's a shame*
> *– it's a shame, it's a crying shame –*
> *Look at those jokers*
> *Glued to the damn hockey game*
> *Hey honey – you've got lots of cash*
> *Bring us round a bottle .*
> *And we'll have some laughs*
> *Gin's what I'm drinking*
> *I was raised on robbery...*

Her lovely grip tightens upon me.
Her heart beats over me.
She lifts me into her voice, we shall never be
this happy again.
She is waking me into herself.
We are flying together.

Terry goes out along the valley's rim, above the marshes and the first stretch of reservoir, handling the curves as if she were in a racing machine. A silver and mother-of-pearl rosary swings from the rear-view mirror, tilting at every corner, a gift from his wife maybe? "She's got what she wants," René always says. Terry's only seen her once, at the party where she and René got together. Elegant, smart, with her own friends. Would she believe he was spending this time with a lab-assistant? Presumably she wouldn't care.

But what the fuck's *she* going to do?

René's been right about so many things. But always the insistence that she'd grow out of him, that he was there to help, but the age difference was too much. Was he right about that too? She used to object to "ma poupée" and "kid", now she accepts them, almost glad to be reminded. And, hot though she is for him still, she *does* notice his aging, his breathless moments, his intolerance of things that still excite her – some of her music.

He's so cool, he laughed or ignored her out of all her games. He taught her things about love, and sex, and herself. It's not so simple, this growing out of someone. And the rotten timing of getting knocked up, half of her not wanting the abortion. And, fuck, he's her only real friend now.

She counts off the signals he's dropped for her:

"So you're not educated, poupée, you don't know much, but you're *smart*."

"You can be tough, Terry, without having to be hard, hein?"

The time he said, "I admire you more than anyone I ever knew. You should admire yourself." "I do admire myself," she'd said, and in that moment it had become true.

And she'd learned how to cry, with him.

Telling him, one time, some of the stuff she'd got into after she'd left home, the people she'd hung out with, and him saying, "You were a *touriste*, Terry, that's all, learning the score. I was the same.

Just passing through and knowing it. Someone like you has *les anges gardiennes*, hein? – guarding angels?"

His gifts to her, like the beads on the rosary in front of her. *Fuck*.

She puts the Van Morrison tape in: "*Take it where you find it*", "*Lost dreams and found dreams in America*". Will another lover ever mean to her what René means. Sometimes so gentle, sometimes unlocking screams from both of their throats. She remembers the cries from her parents' room. When she thought Daddy was beating Mummy up, which made no sense at all in the day to day world. Mummy's pale spite, no real malevolence, her tears when she wanted her way.

The vulgar white nylon dress, "*Far too small for you*", the birthday card, clumsy and illiterate no doubt as the message to René on the seat beside her.

Shiiiiiit!, she yells, banging the wheel, killing Van Morrison dead. This whole trip is pointless.

And then there's the sign: *Lupton. Hartley*. No mileages.

What's she doing? This is just an excuse – she's not going there.

The car slows as she crosses the reservoir dam. The lake is twenty feet below the highwater stain. A couple of kids are walking across, pickerell or walleyes dangling from their hands, steaming in the sun. Native kids, naturally. There's a flock of geese circling overhead, as she climbs the west slope, twenty or thirty of them, tumbling as they reach the lake and then rising again.

The road turns north, through the scant sandhill pastures, and she pulls over at the first gate.

She sits for a few minutes with the engine off, till the heat gets too much, and her thighs start to stick to the seat. She takes a beer with her, climbs the gate and walks slowly till she's out of sight of the road, up the side of a small gully.

There are cactuses everywhere in the sparse grasses – chains of prostrate prickly-pears, and isolated, symmetrical pincushions. God, it's a marginal place.

But it's hot, and the geese are still flying and tumbling, and the sky is completely clear. She lies down by a gopher hole, the ochre sand-tailings; puts the beer aside, closes her eyes, and empties her mind.

> Between heaven and earth
> I unfold beneath her ribs
> I steal through her while she sleeps under
> the sky.

I came in her sleep, she sleeps for me, I sleep
for myself.
She breathes for me, until I can breathe for myself.

She awakes to the sound of breathing. Standing in a circle
around her are five bulls, heads down, only a few feet off. They are
all different colors, they all have rings through their noses. She
leaps up, screaming, waving her arms: "Fuck off! Get lost! Go on —
scoot!" She's terrified.

Then she sees a man coming up the hill. "Easy!" he calls. "They
won't hurt you."

He pushes between a white bull and a skewbald one. They snort
and wheel around and come back. Their amazing, eggplant
testicles. "They're only trouble if there's cows around," he says,
and stoops to pick up her beer bottle, lying spilled by the gopher
hole. "Can't have glass lying around," he says, without accusation.
"Sun shines through it and next thing you know what little grass
we have is up in smoke."

His eyes are blue as the sky. He wears a cowboy hat, boots with
spurs and *chaps*. He's a movie hero, his teeth are white, he's
gorgeous. And he hasn't looked at her tits once. "Hope I'm not
trespassing," she says.

"That depends why you're here," he smiles.

"I was just taking a break from driving."

"Where you headed?"

"I was going to Hartley —"

"Uh huh — I can point you out a short cut."

All the bulls have curls on their brows, like the hair on René's
chest, but silky. "Why do you keep the bulls together? Don't they
fight?"

"Only if there were cows around, and we don't allow them that
privelege. They're our breeding stock — Char'llais", he points to the
white bull, "Simmental", the skewbald, "Limousine — what we call
exotics."

"You mix them all up? Not purebreds?"

"No," he says, and gestures her to follow him down the hill.
"Purebreds are trouble, sooner or later. Mixing the breeds, if you
get it right, gives you a better yield, a healthier herd." She watches
the tapering back, the cute bum. The world is full of beautiful men!
And this one has character — she sees most young guys as pin-ups.

"Which bull would win?" she asks, catching up with him. "If
they did fight?"

"Well," he says. "I suppose the old Simmental – he's got 200 lbs on the others. But this is his last season. He's bologna come September."

"Bologna?"

"That's right," he shrugs, smiling lightly. She can hardly believe a man like this can be so gentle. "Bologna Bulls is what they're called. Just too old and tough even for ground beef."

Suddenly the lazy brute maleness back there seems pathetic. The curls on their brows. "Hey, that's not fair," she says, "just killing them off like that, after what they've done for you. And don't call me city folks, okay?"

He smiles broadly: "As you wish. But you have to be realistic; and they have a good life. A lot of folks would envy them."

She tells herself not to play female games here: "Do you always wear that get up?"

"It's practical," he says, and helps her over the gate. His hand is comfortable, touching a woman – strong but unassertive on her forearm. She makes sure their eyes know each other a moment.

"No gunbelt?"

"Wrong movie," as he swings over the gate. "I don't even hunt antelope."

The geese have swung round again; they come crying over them and tumble through the air with the ragged sound of washing on a windy line. "I've never known them flock up so early," he says. "They must know something we don't."

"Do you hunt *them*?"

He shakes his head: "No, ma'am, not that I've anything against it. But they've been around here longer than I have. Kind of gives a person faith in the Spring coming back." And laughs, with a first hint of self-consciousness.

His pickup is parked behind the Saab. "Nice car," he says. "Another exotic."

"Not mine. It's a friend's."

"Well," he hands her the empty bottle. "I'm Andy Mortensen. We're up at the first farm on the left. You come by again? – drop in. You'll be welcome."

"Okay, and thanks. My name's Terry. Dawson." And she gives him her hand. He's getting crowsfeet already. Character. "Thank you for saving me from the bulls."

"Like I said, they wouldn't hurt you. Only thing to worry about up there would be wood-ticks."

"Oh!" she pulls a face. "Gross!"

"Yep, they even give me the creeps."

"Even you?"

His eyes enjoy the mockery. They slip down to check her hand for rings. He points up the road: "Take the second right," he says. "It's not much of a road but it'll save you a few miles. Maybe twenty minutes drive."

The pickup overtakes her as she reaches the turn-off. She returns his wave and honks twice. The road hasn't been graded all summer; she bottoms out after fifty yards and spends the rest of the drive zigzagging, to keep the wheels on the highest ridges of the gravel.

Her mind separates into its different levels, parallel but sometimes interwoven, like the parts in a music score. It's the thing about her René has never understood, why he so often asks, "Where are you, kid? Qu'est ce que tu pense?" And when she says, "Nothing," it's true, because it's never word-thoughts that he'd understand, or clear memories. He doesn't get her music anyway, the songs that are always the medium her consciousness works through. He only knows the music that she blasts from her stereo, or when they drive together, and then – even when he shares her taste – he tells her "Noise, noise, you kids are just scared of silence."

As part of her steers the low Saab over this obstacle course, another imagines Andy Mortensen submitting to her. Oh we give people something when we give them our names. He must be well into his twenties, but she knows that he's innocent next to her.

At the same time, the songs go on – Chrissie Hynde's voice belting it out inside her – and she realises that's twice today that a man from another world has said, "You'll be welcome." Yes, René's become her whole life; he still has his family, all of his friends intact, but her life's been narrowing down around him. Like when you're in love at 14 and you dump your girlfriends.

"*Don't get me wrong/If I come and go like fashion/I may be great tomorrow/But hopeless yesterday.*" She's only taking this road because Andy was following. The world's waiting, René's right, he's always right. She's not going to stop at Hartley, she's not going to the funeral. "*Don't get me wro-o-o-o-ong/If I phone in a moment of passion/It may not seem believable/But let's not say 'so long'.*" René won't know; she can have the abortion next weekend, and start living again. "*It just might be fantastic/Don't get me wrong...*"

Hartley begins as one street, but forks almost at once into three, with the left branch paved, and a store to the left with gas-pumps by the road. She pulls in, gives the boy who comes out twenty bucks, and goes inside to get cigarettes.

A man is on a ladder, shelving cans that his wife passes up to him. "Where you from?" he says, and climbs down, ready to talk. Terry tells him "Regina" and pays for her smokes. She's fidgetting to get back on the road.

"You got any other kind of money?" the woman asks.

"Sorry?"

"People don't use two dollar bills round here, unless they have to. And I won't get to the bank till Tuesday."

Terry fishes a crumpled ten bill from her jeans. "You having me on?"

The woman takes the bill. "Bad luck," she says. "Two dollar bills come out in the Depression, people just don't like them."

"I always heard it different," the man says. "They're whore bills, if you'll excuse me Miss – two bucks was the price of a whore back then, and that's how the bills got their bad name."

"You learn something every day." Terry pockets the change and strips the cellophane from her cigarettes. And as she lights one at the doorway says, in spite of herself, "You wouldn't know anyone called Metcalfe here, would you?"

The man points across the road: "Name on the mail box," he says.

"We bought this store from Archie Metcalfe," the woman comes out to the door. "He's not a well man, you know – sister come out from England, after his wife died, takes care of him. You connected?"

"On my mother's side, yes. Thought I might look in on them."

The boy is peering in at the Saab's dashboard. "I wouldn't drive up their driveway," he tells her. "It's the pits."

"No, leave it here," the man says.

"Okay, I won't be long. Did you know their daughter?"

"Didn't hear of one," the woman says, "but we only came here five years ago. Or maybe there *was* a girl, was there, Len – got into trouble or something?"

"Something like that," the man looks over his glasses at Terry.

The woman's eyes kindle with interest: "Is that your connection?"

"You got it," say Terry. "I guess I was the trouble." And heads off past the car. "You can move it over for me, can't you?" she winks at the boy. "You bet!" he says and spits, macho, into the dust.

The driveway starts with a mass of lilac bushes, then goes to the left past a dried-up lawn and a jungle of a garden, with a small patch of corn and chrysanthemums and climbing beans. The house is two-storied, weather-bleached and with one porch-gutter down, but it's solid. There's a big shed twenty feet out on the north side, with a rusty weathervane, a rooster, above the door. Even in this heat there's a shimmer of smoke above the house's brick chimney-stack.

Terry stands by the porch. A woman comes round from the south side, arms full of washing, and hesitates, staring in astonishment. "Can I help you?"

"Hi. My name's Terry. I believe my mother grew up in this house."

The woman has a long face, she's about sixty, she has nervous green eyes. "Oh, I don't think so, dear. This house has been in our family for forty two years."

"Maria. Maria Metcalfe?"

"Oh –," the woman stares dreadfully. "Then you –." Her neck flushes.

"I'm her daughter."

Oh. Well, of course, I didn't know her –." The words come out at a rush, the woman seems stranded, stuck with the pile of sheets against her chest. She looks up at the porch, and then back to Terry. "The truth is, my brother's never talked about that. But come on in," she says, "we hardly ever get visitors," and fairly runs up the steps, dumping her laundry onto a wooden bench there. "Come on in, come on. We'll have a cup of tea." And as Terry hesitantly moves: "And don't you mind him – he's had three strokes now and, you know. It was Terry, wasn't it?. Yes. Did you keep the name?"

"Terry Dawson."

"Dawson, yes. Well, that's an English name too, isn't it?" Some of her agitation is taken up by her hands. They are long and much abused by detergents. A thick wedding band on her right middle finger. "My brother can be *cross*," she says, with some defiance.

"Look, I didn't come to cause any trouble for you..."

"No, no, I'm glad of the company. Truly I am. And Archie hardly notices people, or the things that are done for him." There's bitterness too. "My name's Janet. Metcalfe too, of course – I never married."

I am the stone under her heart.

She clenches herself against me, but I will not
let go.

The ripples have stopped, the stone is frozen.

She must take in this air, I have no need for it. I
will sleep and be still.

Her life will warm the stone, it will start to beat,
in spite of her, in spite of this place.

The ripples will go out again, before they close in.

She will know me soon. Soon she will give me my
life.

The television is blaring. The room smells of bread, and
disinfectant and wax polish. The man sits in an upright chair, in
pajamas, a thick cardigan, with a plaid blanket over his knees,
beside the oil cookstove.

His hands are pale as death, wasted versions of his sister's. He
doesn't look up, his chin has a constant tremor through it.

"You just sit down on the couch," the woman fills a kettle at a
sink through the side door. She does everything at a run, talking
the whole time, while the TV blares on, *The Young And The
Restless*, and the old man ignores them both.

Janet Metcalfe brings a milk jug and sugar bowl to the table at
the room's centre. Chattering about the problems with oil stoves,
all the things she had to get used to when she came out to Canada,
the weather. The room is spotless but faded and bare. It has the air
of having been half-cleared out – perhaps to make room for the
invalid. Pictures of English stately homes and landscapes, a Dutch
pendulum clock in the open stairwell. Flowered wallpaper and
brown trim. A varnished plank ceiling. Terry can't see any
photographs.

"Archie," Janet calls, standing by his chair. "Do pay attention
and say hello to Miss Dawson."

His face twists in irritation, he stares round till he fixes on Terry.
His eyes are a similar green to his sister's, but drained and
watering. His jaw-tremor is more pronounced face on, shaking his
lower lip. "Who's this?" he demands.

"Miss Dawson," says Janet patiently, at the top of her voice.
"Terry Dawson. She is –," she hesitates. "Terry is the girl's
daughter, Archie – she's come to see the house."

"My Mother's dead," Terry says. "She died this morning, or last night. I never met her."

"Eh?" the man quavers. His left hand makes little waving motions above the chair arm.

"Maria's daughter, Archie. Maria has passed away."

Terry stares at his face. He seems to be looking through her. Some girl on the TV says "Harold hasn't been home since Tuesday night. I'm out of my mind with worry."

"She was no good!" says the old man. He grips the chair arms and turns himself back to the set. Terry looks up at Janet. "He wouldn't do this" says the TV "unless something was terribly wrong." The old jaw trembles, a line of saliva runs out at the corner of the mouth. Janet dabs at his mouth with a paper towel. "You mustn't mind him," she says, "he doesn't know what he's saying." "No good," the man mumbles, "no good." "Oh Archie," Janet shouts, "be reasonable." "I'm sorry," says an electronic voice, "but your husband has AIDS."

Terry gets up. "I'm going," she says. "I have to get back to town." But Janet has the kettle off the stove and is over by the door at once. "No," she cries, "you mustn't. Not just yet. Let's go for a walk together."

"A walk?"

"Would you like to see your grandmother's grave?" The eyes are desperate with appeal.

"Okay."

They go by a trail through the field out back. "It's heartbreaking for Archie to see the place run down so, but there's only so much I can do." Janet talks on, as if frightened that any silence would find her alone again. "I'm afraid it keeps him even more within doors. He has a wheelchair, but he's never used it since I came. He doesn't like to go out on the veranda even, except some hot nights, after dark."

Terry talks, just to stop the exhausting chatter. "It must have been hard for you, coming out when you did."

"Well he needed me, dear. And our mother had died just a few months before. I looked after her," she says, with a conscious dignity, "for twenty-three years."

"That's awful." Terry stops and turns to her: "You've had no life of your own."

The woman smiles, gratified. "Oh, we mustn't grumble," she says.

"I'd grumble," says Terry. "I'd scream blue murder and tell them where to get off!"

The woman's both pleased and disapproving. They walk on in silence for a couple of minutes, down a lane past the schoolhouse.

The cemetery is small, with two big fir trees at the centre and a carragana hedge all around. There are grasshoppers everywhere among the stones. "We haven't kept things up too well, I'm afraid," Janet says, "but I get a boy to clear the weeds once a month." She points to the stone and stands tactfully back, though she cannot bring herself to leave altogether.

It's polished granite. *To the Memory of Theresa Tekwaysis*, it reads, *Beloved wife of Archibald Metcalfe, 1931–1984*. There is room for his name underneath. Theresa. "Was she his daughter?" Terry asks. "My mother?"

"Oh no, dear," Janet comes close, too close, and looks down at the stone. "No Archibald took her in, and the little one. He was a kind man."

She slips her arm through Terry's. She has the old woman smell of some harsh talcum powder. "Oh, if you'd seen him when he was young," she says, tears starting in her eyes. "We all idolised him. He was the eldest, you see, and the rest of us were girls. And then he went off to Canada, and sent us cards and presents, and then came the war and he was wounded, and we hardly heard from him till his health started failing." She plucks Terry's arm: "Come on back," she says. "I mustn't leave him too long." And then with a gust of sentimental passion: "He deserved better from life than this."

"It must be lonely for you," Terry says, and detaches her arm as they move off. The woman stands for a moment, indulged in the grief that she's raised in herself. There is pain and pride and defiance, all muddled up as "Stay!" she cries, her hand flying out grotesquely, "stay for the night. It *is* lonely. Please say you'll stay." And then hurries up, and says slyly, "You could sleep in your mother's bed."

They eat at the central table, though Archie's chair is turned so he can watch the TV. *Dallas* is playing. Janet sits close beside him, and cuts his food, helps some of it into his mouth, wipes his chin. He ignores Terry, but his sister keeps talking through the TV noise, and scarcely touches her own food. But there's a bottle of gin, and some tonic. Janet encourages Terry to drink, and matches her.

Halfway through the meal Archie lets out a long, burbling fart, and Janet supports him out through the door by the stairwell. God, Terry thinks, never, never, *never*. It's like one of René's mocking scenario's when she first talked about love.

They come back in to the table, Archie oblivious to his sister's exertions, her shaking hands once he's slipped back into his chair. "You know nothing about Dieppe!" he says, glaring at Terry. "Nothing at all." His hand comes up and taps uncontrollably on the table. "Oh, don't start," Janet begs. "He'll ruin his dinner." "Harry Riddell," he says, his eyes accusing, "Harry Riddell. The best friend a man ever had. Harry Riddell." He leans forward at Terry, Janet pulls his plate away from his sleeve. "We got up the beach," he says, his eyes boring into her, "up safe by the sandcliffs, half the regiment dead on the beach behind us. 'We're safe,' I said. And Harry said to me, right there he said

'Oh little did my mother think,
The day she cradled me
That I'd be stormed by shot and shell
To –'

and this shell came in, and he stopped that poem, because his head was blown off. Right then, right beside me."

His jaw trembles, his eyes spring up with tears, there's a terrible wounded beseechfulness about him. Terry reaches over and puts her hand over his. It is dry and cold. "She was no good!" he says, and turns back to *Dallas*.

They have a couple of drinks after Janet puts him to bed, but Terry's energy nosedives. "I've got to sleep," she says. "It's been a crazy day." Janet is too slewed to protest much. "I've put a hot water bottle and fresh sheets on," she says, as if skirting a tongue twister. "You go on up, I've more chores to do." "You should get some sleep too." "No, I don't need much." She pours the last of the gin into her glass. "Goodnight Janet." "Goodnight dear."

Archie's bed is donwstairs, in the old living room. Janet has the main bedroom next to the upstairs bathroom: it's an old fashioned child's room – pink everywhere, flounces around the bedstead, a clutter of ornaments, dolls and photographs. And the smell of that powder she wears.

Terry's room is littered with cardboard boxes, full of preserving jars and gin bottles. Bare plaster walls. The window looks out on the shed, and the weathervane. An empty closet, a bare lightbulb, a narrow bed. But it is warm and soft, though the smell of the hot water bottle is like condoms, and she kicks it out onto the floor.

Gin and exhaustion. She has no time to think about this, her mother's room and bed, to think anything. She curls up on her side, naked, with her hands between her knees, and sleeps.

> I cry. I am the crying she hears, the child weeping inside her dream. I am crying and will not stop. She struggles to escape into the light. My tears are embedded in her own moaning. She is desperate to come awake.
>
> She knows me. She has heard me before.

She's awake. Something fell over. She can hear arguing in the next room. A man's voice rises to a shout, a woman's wailing, there's an exclamation, a smacking blow, and someone staggers against furniture.

"No-ohh," she hears the woman's voice.

Then a door dragged open.

"No!" the voice is clear now. "No, you mustn't!" Tears and pain in the cry. "Please come back!"

It's too dark to see anything. Foreboding trembles up through her. She stretches up for the light cord, has to kneel up to reach it. There's stumbling on the landing, a man's raging, "Get back, woman – get back to bed!"

Her bedroom door opens softly. There's a man there, looking at her. He wears a blue dressing gown. He gestures violently as a woman grabs at his left arm.

"Get off!" he shouts. His voice is flat, and echoes in the room. Terry feels the hopeless sobs beginning in her stomach. She can see the woman, short and dark, in a white nylon nightdress, her hair wild. "Don't!" she cries, tugging again at the man's arm. "You promised! Please, honey, come back to bed!"

The top of the man's dressing gown is pulled open. He twists to free himself and his other arm goes up. The sound of the blow is like firewood splitting. The woman falls out of sight. He comes in and closes the door.

She crosses her hands over her chest. The whimpering is trapped in her throat. She sits by her pillow, unable to move. Down the centre of his chest is a scar like a zipper, grey.

He stares at her. She cannot stop the whimpering. She reaches up and pulls the light-cord.

The ripples go out.
We possess each other.

The crying stops. Terry's awake again. She sits bolt upright, and tears the wet bedsheets away from herself.

Her heart is panicking, her tongue is numb – she was biting it.

"Shit!" She flings her legs out of bed and stands, unsteady. She threads her way through the litter of boxes and bottles, and drags the window up. It falls back with a crash. She gets one of the bottles and props it open.

There's already some light in the sky. The air is dry and still warm, there's the smell of wolf-willow. Everything is still.

She looks directly out at the weathervane on the shed roof. As her mother must have looked out at it. Her hands go up to her swollen nipples. "Sweet jesus," she tells the night.

She goes back and sits on the bed. Do they lock the house? She'll never get back to sleep now. Her heart is still racketting. She lies back again in the half dark, her hands behind her head.

Then Janet is at the door. "Terry, I brought you some coffee" her eyes avert from the girl's nakedness. "It's ten o'clock, dear. Did you sleep well?"

When Terry comes down, he's by the stove again, but the TV's still off. "I'm really late," she tells Janet. "I have to leave right away."

"You'll come back and visit?" the long face is grey and pathetic.

"Maybe," says Terry. "Anyway, thanks for the hospitality."

"It's a joy," Janet says. "It's a joy to have visitors."

The old man has not looked up. He stares at the blank TV, jaw trembling, hands loose and white on the chair arms. There's a streak of spittle on his cheek, Janet reaches for a paper towel. "No let me." Terry takes the towel and dabs at his face, the spittle hangs over the sparse white bristles.

"You are a dear," Janet says. "Will you say goodbye, Archie?"

Terry gets hold of his pajama lapels, and pulls him straighter in the chair. He is almost weightless. She looks into the faded eyes, and tugs him a little closer. There's a flicker of fear there. She pulls the lapels wider, a button comes away. Just enough to see the top of the scar, a grey zipper pattern on the loose flesh of his chest. She releases him. "Goodbye, Father," she says quietly. The eyes stare drearily into hers.

At the end of the dead lawn she turns and sees Janet on the

porch, bent over and peering out at her through the sunlight. It's
roasting hot already. Terry waves. Janet doesn't seem able to see
her.

The keys are still in the car. She drives off without looking in at
the store. "Son of a bitch," she says to herself, "son of a bitch, son of
a bitch."

The beer is warm, but she opens one anyway, drinks and lights a
cigarette. "Alright, kid," she says to herself. "I know the rules.
This is my last pack."

She pushes the tape in the cassette. Van the Man still, moaning
and saying 'yeah' and 'alright' over some fiddle and guitar track. A
voice out of René's world.

"But listen," she says, settling the bottle between her thighs,
"One hour after you're born, one damn hour, I'm lighting up again.
Okay?"

She's out of town, following a sign for Fort Qu'appelle. The beer
is sticky on her lips. She cranks up the sound; the speakers jounce
by the back seat:

> *"Then we'll walk down the avenue again*
> *And we'll sing all the songs from way back*
> *when*
> *Yes we'll walk down the avenue again*
> *When the healing has begun..."*

A piano joins in with the tune, lifting the tempo.

"We're in this together, kid," she says, and picks up speed
towards the valley. "You just better be a girl!"

Saturday, 12.25 and he sees the dust cloud coming fast down the
22nd. He backs the cruiser off the highway, and waits.

The car doesn't see him till it rounds the bend, 200 yards back. In
his mirror he sees the driver reach quickly sideways and down. The
car slows as it approaches. A woman, no passengers.

He turns on the roof-lights, puts on his hat, and steps out.

The grey Saab pulls up behind the cruiser. The girl has black
hair to her shoulders, dyed on one side with a peacock-blue flash, a
full, pretty mouth. "Any problem?" she says. There's a sassy look
about her.

"Just checking, Miss," he says. He eyes the *Miller* case on the
seat beside her. "Would you mind turning the music down, Miss?"
Grasshoppers are banging into his boots and pinging off the car,

masses of them out of the dry roadside grasses, like soft green bullets.

"You wouldn't have any open liquor in there, would you?"

The girl takes off her shades and grins up at him. Her eyes are a striking pale green, she's a beauty. She shakes her head. Her purse is on the floor by the passenger seat; he can see the beer stain spreading through it.

"May I see your licence?"

She reaches down, registers the spill, tries to dig out her wallet without exposing the bottle.

"Come on, Lady," he says. "You don't want to ruin everything in your purse. Bring it out."

She shrugs resignedly, hands him out the wallet and sneaks a last sip from the bottle before he takes it from her and empties the dregs on the road.

She dodges a grasshopper and rolls up her window. He walks round, checking the car over, and motions her to unlock the passenger door. When he's halfway back to the cruiser with the beer-case, she calls out. "What do you do with the stuff?"

He opens the trunk. "We dispose of it."

Yeah, I bet!" She's standing by her car.

"That's what they all say. It's like a record." He slams the trunk. "Now, would you bring your registration, and come to my car?"

He calls in her licence number. No record. She gets in beside him and picks up his hat from the seat.

"Who is René Lauzon?"

"A friend." She twirls the hat on her finger. Her perfume is delicate, classy.

"Does he know you're out here?"

"Look, Buffalo Man," she says. "I'm not a car-thief. Of course he knows."

He reaches for his hat; "Buffalo man?"

She twirls the cap, out of his reach, and points to the RCMP badge. Her eyes dare him to relax. She's cute, alright, and she's not wasting time getting mad at him.

"What'll it cost me?" she asks, and she puts his hat on, and moves his rearview mirror to admire herself in it. She tucks her hair back behind her ears: "Do you think they'd have me?"

"In the force?"

"Sure – I can ride a horse."

He laughs. "It wouldn't hurt our image," he says. "The ticket's for fifty dollars if you pay on time."

"Can I keep just one of the beers?"

"Are you serious? Now just give me my hat –"

"Hey, I'm going to a funeral. Got to keep my spirits up."

"Where's the funeral?"

"Lebret. My mother."

"I'm sorry," he says. He looks at her curiously: "I wouldn't have took you for a native." Though with those cheekbones, the hair – only the eyes don't fit.

"I didn't know I was, till yesterday."

"That the truth?"

"Mm hmm. She asked for me just before she died. Weird eh?"

He hands her back the papers. "You can sign on the back of this, Teresa, if you want to plead guilty –"

"It's Terry."

"Alright. Or you can contest it, on the date shown – there."

"Can I keep a beer?" Her eyes tease, but they don't put him on the spot.

"I'm not looking," he says. She touches his shoulder and grins again. She has wonderful, even teeth. He looks out the window; she has the grace not to let the bottle clink.

"Thanks, Buffalo Man," she says, and gets out.

She walks with a sort of lifting step. Happy. She's sexy as hell in her white cotton pants.

"Hey!" he leaps out of the car, all his police paranoia back in place. "You come right back here, right now!" His hand even feints towards his holster.

She has her car door open. She waves his hat at him: "I'm not stealing it," she yells. "Honest, I'll be right back."

She reaches into the Saab, squats down on the road and then stands, slamming the door. She comes back towards him. He gets back in.

She comes to the passenger door. "Sorry," she smiles. Her shades are back on. "Just wanted to get a rise out of you. I like you, Buffalo Man."

"Alright," he says. "Just give me my hat."

She sets it down carefully on the seat.

"Maybe see you again," he says.

"Not in the line of business, I hope. Yeah, well you never know. Bye."

He says, "Watch how you drive, Terry," as she slams the door.

The Saab drives past. She smiles and waves. He nods.

A nice encounter, he thinks. There's still a trace of her perfume in the cruiser. He picks up the hat. Three grasshoppers fly out of it into his face.

He swats them out the window, and leans back in his seat. He is smiling broadly in spite of himself. It's the first time since he was posted here that he hasn't felt like a cop.

He sits for a while, listening to the hopper bombardment of the cruiser, watching her dust.

The Saab crosses the highway and heads straight for Qu'Appelle. But then he sees the dust settle near the 10th. After a minute, it starts up again, veering to the right, picking up speed along the valley side.

Well, the little cow, he thinks. Wherever she's going, it sure as hell isn't to Lebret.

Running on
Empty

YESTERDAY WE WENT INTO LETHBRIDGE and run into Jack
Bishop. Dar amd me were just loading what seemed like
a half ton of parcels into the pickup when someone
yelled "Hey Piper, how's tricks!" and there he was on the
sidewalk, in new shoes and permapress pants, and his face and
bald head pink with the cold.

First time I believe I ever saw him without his hardhat on. Used
to wear it in the office, feller said Jack kept it on when he took a
shower.

"Not bad Jack," I said, "How about yourself?" And he came over
and leaned on the box-side. "Couldn't be better," he said. "Me and
the old lady patched things up and we're in to do some Christmas
shopping."

"Uh huh," I said. He looked the pickup over. "Nice old rig you
got," he said, "Cornbinder eh? Run okay do she?" "Runs fine," I
said. "She's all I got to show for a summer's work, but I could've
done a lot worse."

Dar's putting some bags in the cab and he's looking her over too.
Course, Dar dresses like a hooker, that's her style, and I've no
complaints about that, but Jacky was getting his eyeful. Right
then his old lady come out of the store behind him. A biggish
woman in a rabbit skin jacket, with a baby in a pink jumpsuit on
one arm and a big store bag in the other.

Jack scurried over to take the bag, and made the introductions.

77

"Gooday, maam," I said. "Pleased to meet you Mr Piper." Folks is more or less like dogs, I suppose – there's more going on in the way of sniffing and looking and how you hold your head than anything actually gets said.

She had a thin mouth and a heap of mascara, and her eyes were saying "You and me is equals, feller, and you and me both know I've got a loser here, and you and me both know I've put one over on him." Truth is, though, in a funny sort of way she looked kind of like Jack, but then they were married close to 15 years I believe, before she effed off on him.

"Best cruiser we ever had on the claim," Jack chimes in, which was a pile of horseshit given the circumstances. "What you working at now, Piper?"

I told him me and Dar were sitting a farm over the winter. "Grain farm," I said, "just a few horses and barns to look after."

His wife looked in the cab at Dar, who'd settled in and got her country station ripping out – Dar don't go for the social niceties when she sees no call for it. And all I can say about that woman's look when her eyes come back to me is it was reproachful. Like "a man like you wasting time on young flesh when a real woman could be available." I guess women really don't like to see a man with a young girl, it brings out disapproving looks in them, and I have to say I got an allergy to being disapproved of. Never did get used to it.

Off she went towards their car and Jack give me a little wink, and jerked his head towards the cab. "That your daughter, Piper?" he said, and give me a man to man look. Trouble is, Jack don't cut it as a good old boy, and them kind of cracks fall flat coming from him. I was so gracious not to say "No Jacky boy, is that *your* daughter?" since it obviously weren't *his* baby they had with them. Either the get of buddy she took off with, or one of his successors.

But I just smiled easy and got in the cab and said "Be seeing you Jack."

"No hard feelings Piper," he said, "about last Spring I mean?" "Why no Jacky," I said. "Best thing that ever happened to me." I put her into gear, radio was playing, *I want to settle down but they won't let me*, Dar's kind of music. I tipped my hat and rolled down the window. "You tell Denny I did try working for myself," I said. "Didn't quite work out but I'll get the hang of it." And drove off.

Dar was fixing her face in a hand mirror. "What was that all about?" she said. Thing with Dar is, she always plays the radio so goddam loud I have to guess what she's saying half the time. Don't bother me though – I just filter it out and think my own thoughts when we're on the road. Together and apart, that's how to keep things easy. No music or thoughts ever stopped two bodies in a cab *touching* each other.

"That was Jack Bishop," I said, "Brother of the feller I worked for before I came down from the hills and met you." She pinched that mouth of hers – don't know why she has to plaster it with pink goop all the time, but I've kind of got used to the slippy feel and candy taste. Likely I'd miss it if she quit. "I thought they fired you," she said. "That's right, and aren't you glad?" She slid over against me, "Uh huh," she said and pinched my thigh inside, just lightly but it can really hurt a guy, it's a trick she learned in Calgary. "Three nights without you Piper," she said, dreamily, "how am I going to make out?" "Why," I said, "you planning to make out with someone?" and she laughed and swatted me across the side of my head, cause Dar puts everything into everything she does, and that's the truth, and so we drove on up 19 and out on the 12th and she dropped me at the farm gate and give me a long kiss and said, "Save yourself for Sunday, lover," and off she went with that load of presents for her family, and the Cornbinder turned off at the end of the concession, and I had the world to myself for three days.

That has to be the most words I ever set down on paper since I quit school. I mean, for all folks laugh at me for the stuff I *read*, bar maybe one letter a year to Joannie and the kids I don't believe I ever filled up a page in the last 20 years.

I guess it's like talking to yourself, only you don't catch yourself off guard like a stranger was watching. And it eats up the time, it sure does that. It was barely dark when I started in last night, and damned if the clock on the stove didn't say 11.30 when I quit. Near six hours gone missing without a trace, except for these five old elevator receipts covered with words, and I didn't get up once from the kitchen table, not even for a cup of coffee or to take a leak.

Now it looks like I'm back in the saddle again, so I'll fix it down, the clock's saying ten of three and the sun's just hit the poplar bluff in the back forty. This being Friday.

Course I planned to spend this time alone *reading*, not writing, only I forgot when Dar dropped me off that my new books were in back with her presents, not in the cab with the groceries, so she took off to Palliser with all my reading material except the one

Equinox magazine I had in my jacket pocket, and I pretty well had that read through in the coffee shop, waiting on her shopping.

It was kind of strange, walking through the barn and the driving shed yesterday, dumping out hay for the horses and a hatful of oats apiece. Nothing else moving except the collie dog by the back door and the barn cats. Must be nine or ten of them, but the cold'll take care of most of them. There's one old Tom, though, grey, with his ears and tail froze off in other winters. Sat glaring down at me from on top of the grain locker, like a mean old lynx. I did think of taking one of the quieter horses out for a run, I'm no great horseman but there's frost enough in the ground to make the going easy. There's one yellow gelding called Snooze, and I fancied getting out on the stubbles with him and clear my head. Maybe tomorrow.

Seems I've lost the habit of just being alone with myself. But plenty that's new has gone down this last half year, and seeing Jack Bishop again got me thinking it through.

Now you'd have to say that Jacky Bishop was a weak man, which is funny when you think he had to do any dirty work there was going. Like firing me, for instance. His brother Denny could've looked any man straight in the face with those blue eyes of his and said, Well I'm laying you off and no hard feelings unless you want to make them hard, and if you need a reference I'll give you one without telling no lies, and if you plan to get mean about it I'll bust you out through that glass door here and now, so what you say? Okay, here's your severance, shake, goodbye. And get back to the job.

Which in Denny's case was hands-on stuff, in the mill shed, but for reasons best known to him he gave Jacky charge of accounts, maintenance and personnel.

So I got word that morning to go to the accounts shack. Where he pushed a few bills around on the desk and then told me the glad tidings.

I was standing and he was sat behind his desk, which was his mistake. Like, whenever a cop pulls me over I'm out of my vehicle like a flash, and back and standing by his door, looking down through his window and saying "What's the problem?" It's what you'd call a moral advantage I guess. Sort of top dog. Guess there's the odd City cop it wouldn't work on though.

I said "Why?"

"I'm not saying I altogether go along with this, Piper," he said, and his eyes didn't come no taller than my belly button, "but it's out of my hands, so I'm sorry but that's how it is."

I said "Why?"

He looked up at me, like it's him getting fired, not me, and then he starts swinging back and forward on his spring-loaded office chair and he said, "You know how it is, Piper. The feeling is you don't, like, fit in with the rest of the operation." Him and Denny were both hot on that word, *operation*. "Like you know," he said and shrugged his shoulders inside his softball jacket, "myself I believe in live and let live, long's a feller does his job, how he is otherwise don't count, but –

"How am I otherwise?" I said.

He'd lost his thread by them. "Don't give me a hard time, Piper," he said, "we all know you can twist out of an argument like a coon hound –"

"I ain't arguing," I said, "but this here's a crock of shit and you know it. Half the outfit barely speaks the language, you put up with Birdie Daniel, goes AWOL for days at a time – what'd I do that's such a problem?"

"Don't push me," he said, "I got a job to do." Jack's mouth is too small though it could've been kind of pretty when he was young and the stuffing hadn't been knocked out of him. In fact that mouth is the one thing him and his brother had in common. Anyways, now he'd dropped the confidential tone – Jack would always conspire with you if he thought it'd work, but watch out if he needed to cover his own ass.

You can work today, and Friday if you want," he said, "but we'll pay you to the week's end anyways. Holiday pay too, of course."

"Listen Jack," I said, "I was planning on settling in. Even talked to a feller about renting a place."

He acted deaf and kept talking. "Brenda's got it figured out and a cheque made out for you." And he reached down to pull a drawer open. I hate it when a guy puts on weight that way and his jacket and shirt come loose from his belt – I reckon that bit of flesh above the ass is the ugliest thing on a man like that.

He come up with a envelope and said, "If you want a ride out today, Craven's taking some bushings in for retooling. I told him to wait for you."

"Nice to be the first to know about it," I said. "You got a smoke there, Jack?" He was always supposed to be giving up but he fished a pack of Export from under a catalogue and pushed them over. "Keep them," he said, "I won't be needing them. Need a light?" He bent down again – there was a blonde on the calendar, on her knees in the sand, and Jack's face purple in front of her from the exertion of reaching for a match. Getting flabbier every week, seemed to me, but like my sister said to me one time – fat men are just like rats trying to eat their way out of a trap. Joannie's pretty smart for someone with a college degree, and I said "What about fat women, Joannie?" and she laughed and said, "They know there's no way out, they just eat to sustain the boredom."

So I said I'd go right away. Didn't take me long to pack my clothes and stuff but I told Jack I'd need to leave some boxes of books and magazines till I was settled, and he laughed and said they'd take care of the library, and I cleared out my room in the bunkhouse and went down to the marshalling yard.

The green three-quarter ton was idling by the gate, and Jacky was talking to Craven and as I got to them Denny came out of the sorting shed and yelled to me. He come across the yard, walking like a bantamweight, with just that little drag to his left leg from the accident. I guess when Jack's old lady effed off and left him with the two girls he knew he could count on Denny – that's why he come home, stead of making one for himself, but it was sure hard figuring them both coming out of the same matrimonial embraces.

"Your off then Piper," says Denny and he fixes me with those blue doll eyes like he was good-naturedly just *hoping* I'd make trouble. Denny's the kind of feller gives free enterprise a good name, and like all his sort he's always dead certain about how things work and what he has to say about them. But I liked him cause he was still open to learning new stuff, in fact he wasn't close minded at all. Denny's no more a redneck than I am.

"Looks that way Denny," I said, and I flung one of my bags in beside the bushings.

"Your a hard worker, Piper," he said, "but you're not a good worker."

"Yeah?" I said.

"If I were you," he said, "I'd start working for yourself. You'd do alright, and you'd settle in so's your energy wouldn't go to waste."

I laughed, but I figured he had a point.

From where we were stood there was a view out over fifty miles of prairie, dry-brown even this early in May, and nothing in the sky but four or five small clouds high up, drifting towards us. And I laughed again, I guess.

"Tell you what, Denny," I said, "I'll lay you an extra week's wages I can make that cloud up there disappear."

He looked up, they all did. "Which one?" he said.

"That one" – I pointed to the one heading straight for us. "That one shaped like a hound dog," and he said "Your on." And him and his brother both leaned on the gate, grinning from ear to ear, and Craven climbed out from the cab.

The cloud was coming over not too slow and I commenced staring. It's a trick I learned from an old bohunk used to do it at the rodeos when I was a kid. I don't mean he told me no secret – I just figured it out watching him. He'd do it for 10 bucks a time and folks would chip in to challenge him, and if you pick the right dry day, and the right kind of smoke-puff cloud not moving too slow, then making that cloud vanish is child's play.

So I stared and the cloud came on and it was thinning and stretching out and then there were tears in it and tatters, and then it broke in two and the two bits commenced shrinking and I heard Denny laugh and Craven say "son of a bitch" cause they could see I was going to do it and then the cloud was gone.

"How'd you do it," Jack asked.

"Animal magnetism," I said. "How's about that week's wages, Denny?"

Denny seemed purely delighted by the whole transaction. "Didn't you give him his cheque Jack?" he said.

"I got it here," I said, and tapped my back pocket.

"You didn't look at it yet?"

"I'd no reason not to trust you," I said.

He laughed out loud and moved off from the fence. "There's a bonus week's pay in there anyways," he said. Denny just never seemed to be knocked off balance.

"Guess I just earned it then," I said.

He laughed and punched my shoulder and headed off across the yard.

Me and Craven went through town so's I could cash my cheque at the Credit Union and then we set off the two hour drive down from the hills. "What'll you do next?" he asked me. "I don't know," I said. "I believe I'll stay clear of the city. Maybe there's something behind this move I don't understand yet, maybe it's predestined."

Craven was alright I guess but he was enjoying me getting the boot, that's certain. He let out a guffaw like we had an audience in the cab to side with him. "Where you dig them words up Piper?" he said.

"Ain't nothing wrong with words," I said. "New words is new knowledge."

"And see where it gets you," he said.

"Nothing like new words for humbling a man," I said.

"I aint humbled and I aint fired," he said, and we mostly listened to the radio till he dropped me at the Lethbridge bus depot.

There was a bus going west via Calgary in about an hour, and there was an Edmonton bus leaving at 3.30 but bus depots are the dregs, though there's food for thought to be found everywhere, I won't deny that, only I done all the thinking I plan to do in the dregs department five years back, so I took the one long-distance bus that as waiting to go – heading east to Swift Current Saskatchewan and connections, so I bought a ticket for there and see where that pointed me. Only I didn't get near that far of course and I still got the unused part of that greyhound ticket somewhere.

It was high noon by the time we were clear of the irrigation belt and from then on it was a sad sight cause those prairie farms were parched to nothing. After the first stop there wasn't more than ten or twelve people on the bus and I turned the air on my face and semi-dozed with my head against the window. Old feller in the seat ahead caught my eye like he wanted to engage in conversation, but he wasn't pushy and I kept heading him off by shutting my eyes and pulling my hat down, till this preacher come on the radio station talking about the drought and flood and famine the world over, and how the grasshoppers that finished last year's crops off was a plague of locusts and how it was all the bible prophecies coming about. Then the old feller heaved around in his seat and said to me it was hard not to think there might be something in all that.

I couldn't resist him talking to me direct, so I pushed my hat back and he had lively eyes and you could see he'd been an active man, so I straightened up and said, "You mean about the plague of hoppers and all?"

And he said, "Well what do you make of it?"

Well it's sort of a hobby horse of mine so I did tell him what I thought. I told him what I read in this book called "The Doomsday Book" all about extinct animals, and how there was this bird once they called the Eskimo Curlew, that nested somewheres in the

Arctic, no one ever found where. And these birds, in their millions, would migrate down the Atlantic coast to South America and then come Spring they'd fly back north again, this time across the Great Plains. And people just killed them in their millions, like the buffalo and that passenger pigeon, until in a few years they were all gone.

The Eskimo name for them meant The Whistlers, which I happen to know is that they also call the Northern Lights, though that wasn't in the book.

So I told the story, and then what the pay-off was, the book said the birds would settle on the prairies on the way north and cover acres of land, which was when they got shot off and netted and knocked down with sticks, and what they were doing was they were gorging themselves on Rocky Mountain Grasshoppers.

That's what it said in the book, but what it didn't say, which I also worked out for myself, is that us killing off them birds is what left us stuck with hoppers periodically. Which maybe you could see as God's justice, I said.

And I told him how I read in Equinox magazine last year how someone claimed to have seen three Eskimo Curlew in the Carribean somewhere, and I said so maybe things can heal, you know, or if not heal maybe things just come around again.

Guess I rattled on for a little while, I did notice one or two folks across the aisle tuning in and out, but I said my say and towards the end the old feller's eyes were twinkling and this little grin kept pulling at his lips though he didn't take his eyes from mine once.

"You do talk a blue streak, son," he said.

"I been told," I said, but I was feeling pretty well-disposed, like it was clear he was enjoying himself. "I just aint used to folks listening so well."

"At my age," he said, "your grateful for anyone talking to you – to you or at you, you're grateful." And then he laughed and said, "You got an audience, son, keep her coming."

But I guess I'm a sprinter, not a distance talker, so I sort of dried up politely and started looking out the window, till we come to the edge of the next town, with a little river, near parched up, and we had to wait on four or five big cattle trucks at the junction, and the old feller said to me that this would be a ghost town soon – ranchers selling off their cattle and no crop to speak of for three years, no snow, no rain, he said this could be Palliser's last year.

There was a little girl standing by the road, not watching the bus or the cattle transports. If I ever saw an oblivious person it was her. Just stood, staring back at the green hills, lips parted and her little hands hung still and open by her side. She was maybe seven or eight, I don't know why she matters here, but she does. She made me wish I was a father and glad I wasn't at the same time.

The driver took a break and I had a coffee in the hotel with the old feller and he told me I should write a book. "Why everything I know comes out of books," I said, and he said yes, but wasn't that true for everyone and it was how you *connected* things and told them, like some people can tell jokes and others can't.

When the driver got up to pay his check it came to me that I'd stay, cause when we'd left the bus I just liked the feel of the place, and how the hills and the maples by the river side were the same height. So I got my bags off the bus and said

Well, there's the story of how I got to Palliser and my pen ran out then which is no surprise when I see how much I've written, and I pretty near had those old elevator receipts used up too.

It was near 9.30 when I left off, which takes some beating, and it's pushing midnight now and I won't write much more tonight only I can't resist starting in on this new book I've got to write in.

Cliff and Dorrie Sprintz were just over from the next spread. I guess they wondered why the pickup wasn't out front. Asked us round for Boxing Day and told me more than I needed to know about the trials and tribulations of the Wilsons, who own this place. Leastways, Dorrie told me. Cliff's pretty quiet socially. Good enough people, anyways.

Dar thinks the farmers' wives are real funny. She said Dorrie's always bitching about Cliff feeling her up in the kitchen when she's trying to get his dinner cooked, but I wonder how she'd feel if he stopped. It's weird the stuff women tell each other.

Anyways, Dorrie seems to know the inside of this house as well as her own, and when I said I wanted some paper, to write letters I said, she went straight into the daughter's room, where there's a desk with a computer on and stuff, and she opened a drawer and there was three or four empty school books, and a bunch of bic pens too, but the funny thing was, when she was at the desk I looked up and there was that old Tom cat from the barn, staring in at the window with his ugly face so close to the glass it was misting round his nose, and his mouth was half open and his eyes boring in.

Sounds funny, I guess, but that hard bitten face gave me the creeps because I'd seen that look before, the time my uncle and me squared off, and that smile of his. I knew what it meant, clear as words. It meant "Alright you little son of a bitch, this time I've got an excuse and your going to find out what the world's really about." I was near wetting my drawers, and I flung the can of oil at him and ran, and I kept running and none of them heard from me again till I went to see Joannie seven years later, who was married then and had the babies and weren't divorced yet.

The Sprintzes left, after Dorrie had made tea for us all and fished out some cookies and washed a few dishes I had in the sink, and I sent Cliff off with a few Equinox magazines, because he likes the National Geographic, and I gave him "The Silent Spring" by Rachel Carson, though he said he was an awful slow reader , which is a great book, only it seems to me it was written twenty five years ago and ten million people bought it and no one did dick all about it.

To get back to Palliser, I got a room at the hotel – I remember I asked for a room with a view which they thought was a big laugh cause they never thought of their burg as a beauty spot, but I told them I'd come from the hills and sort of missed them. Then I went and walked along the river and stretched my legs and thought a bit, come back and had a bite to eat and went into the bar. Fair crowd of people there, pool table, Kenny Rogers on the juke box, usual thing.

I sat with my beer and the local paper, figuring I'd have to find work and lodgings if I was going to stay, only I couldn't read in there. I don't know why people have to drink in the dark, but it seems they do.

I listened, and they were a cheerful crew, making light of their troubles and I was picking up on my thoughts from when I was walking. You'd think in these desperate times that people would sit quiet once in a while and figure things out for themselves, be still like that little girl on the edge of town, but no they just keep moving faster and talking louder and trusting that things'll be taken care of. Whether it's cancer, or pollution, or the weather or their debt to the harvester dealership, they just figure it'll get taken care of. And I thought, that's just faith on their part, blind faith and optimism, and I thought, people in the Dark Ages so called didn't put near so much faith in the priests and God as we put in scientists and luck, for all the evidence that's staring us in

the face. And I dipped my finger in my beer and wrote it on the table
WE ARE A CREDULOUS PEOPLE, A PREY TO
SUPERSTITION
cause when those words come to
me I got to write them somewhere, can't rightly say them to
anyone.

Then I took the paper over to the shuffleboard table which was
vacant just then and well lighted, and a man in a brown suit came
over and introduced himself, Jake Merrilees, and asked where I
was heading, and when I said I planned to stay if there was work he
said the only person who'd find work in Palliser would be a
rainmaker.

"I can make rain," I said. Or like, the words said themselves.

"You can?" he said. "You got that cloud-seeding gear with you?"
I said no, I just had the gift.

"My family's been finding wells and making rain for three
generations," I said.

"They ain't exactly the same thing," he said. But I told him it
was just finding water, upstairs or down, I could do it.

Now first you have to understand that when I find words forming
themselves in me like that, I've learned to give them their head.
Oftentimes my words have a better angle on things than I do.
Sometimes they're out of line and it leads to trouble, but not that
often.

The other thing is that this must just sound like BS written down
this way, but I've got a way about me sometimes and when I'm *on*
people trust me. Got nothing to do with me, so I don't question it.
Just I nearly always know when I'm *on*. Other times folks just
yawn in my face and I dry up.

Jake Merrilees gave me some droll looks, but he had a mouth
made everything seem droll. He was a surveyor and insurance
agent and he said I should come to the cattlemen and grain-raisers'
meeting tomorrow afternoon if I was serious. He didn't ask too
many questions, just I told him they'd nothing to lose, I only
charged for results. And he said that every farmer in that little
valley stood to lose $30,000 minimum if the rain stayed away one
more year. "How many in your association?" I asked. And he said
45.

I went to bed thinking I could do alright financially if I could
trust this idea.

And going to bed is what I've got to do now.

Dar called this morning. I heard the phone when I was in the barn and guessed it was her. Sure enough she called back ten minutes after. She is sure an uncomplicated creature, aint got a self-conscious bone in her body. She was in a great mood, said the kids had got into their presents before she was out of her coat, never mind waiting for Christmas Day, and they'd opened *my* present from her too and they thought it was a door-stopper. So I know what that means – either she bought me the two volume dictionary with the magnifying glass, or else its that big Columbia encyclopedia. I hope it's that. How I am is just fine with Dar, though it don't make much sense to her. Guess I'm the same with her. True love, if it lasts.

And she said one young couple in Palliser wanted me to stand godfather for their first baby due next February, which is a hoot; and she wanted to bring her little sister Cheryl down for Christmas if I didn't mind. I said why would I mind? And she chattered on, and by the sound of it everyone at the other end was having a great time, and she asked me what I'd been up to.

I said the Sprintzes were over and asked us for Boxing Day, and I told her about the old Tom cat and how he'd followed me from the barn and rolled on the doorstep and nearly come inside and the dog was going nuts on its chain. And I said seemed like I was working on a book.

"Will I be in it?" she said.

"Aint reached that bit yet," I said.

"Jeez I'm horny Piper," she said.

I told her I hadn't given that a thought. "But now you mention it," I said.

Dar's great. One time I went into town and she had a candle burning for me in the window. Knocked me out. Uncalculating affection will do that to a man. Joannie'd get a laugh out of hearing me say that! She'd tell me to hoe a straight row too, so I'd best get back to it.

There was forty or more farmers and ranchers in the hall and a few of their wives too, they'd been listening to some provincial official and they were drinking coffee and standing round in groups when Jake Merrilees introduced me. I wasn't any too eloquent as it turned out. Just told them my name and that I figured I could make rain fall for them, and I said it wasn't science and technology but it weren't witchcraft neither and if any of them were church going people they should have no qualms. And I said what I'd told Jake the night before, that they couldn't really lose, because no rain, no pay, all I wanted was a vehicle and a couple blankets and permission to go anywhere in the valley I chose. And give me three weeks.

No one got too excited, but Jake said if it came to that I could use his old pickup and why didn't I stretch my legs for ten minutes while they talked it over.

I went across the street and browsed around the hardware store, which wasn't doing a great trade but it smelled like hardware stores used to smell, and I bought a kettle and an enamel mug, and then when I went outside there was an old chevvy station wagon parked there and someone yelled "Hey Rainmaker, come over here!"

There was a native feller at the wheel, about 35 I'd say, in fact the car was full of natives, youngsters mostly. "Word travels fast," I said.

The driver was one of those big-faced Indians and he had a grin on that face and he said "What's a white man doing, trying to make rain? We're the people got that knowledge."

Now I do know a fair bit about natives, I've read a lot, starting with "Bury My Heart At Wounded Knee" by Dee Brown ten years ago. And I know the Bloods were part of the Blackfoot Confederacy and the Blackfoot were like the Zulus in Africa – rapers and pillagers on the move who were unlucky enough to get on a roll at the exact same time as the Europeans.

"Come on Chief," I said, "What did you Bloods have to do with the weather, 'cept to get your tents up before the snow came."

"Aint no chiefs here," he said, "and I'm an Apache."

"I'm impressed," I said. "You must find it a mite chilly here in Canada." Which got a laugh from most of them. "And my name's Piper," I said, "not Rainmaker. What's yours?"

"Rufus Skylight," he said. He couldn't have made that up.

"Well I tell you chief," I said, and I looked up over the houses.

"No chiefs here," he said.

"Just a way of speaking," I said. "Nothing but respect intended." They were all laughing anyway. "Tell you what," I said, "You see that cloud up there, that one shaped like a whale?"

He lowered his window some more and looked up. "Looks more like a weasel to me," he said. "Yeah, maybe you're right," I said, "and I'll bet you a sawbuck I can make that cloud disappear before your very eyes. Just so you'll know I'm weatherwise."

They all craned through the windows at the cloud. One of the smoke-puff variety I mentioned before.

"Okay," said Rufus. "Your on."

So I set down my parcel and hunkered down against his door and stared at the cloud. Trouble was, that car was burning oil, and the tailpipe was rusted out and the exhaust was blowing across my face. And Rufus said no he didn't believe he would turn the engine off – you never knew if it might not start again. And the radio was bellowing forth of course – the worst kind of country music, meaty sherrif voices singing about home cooking and heartburn all at the same time and playing guitar through their noses, and he wouldn't turn that down neither. And one of the youngsters had his hand out the window. slapping it on the roof in time to the music right above my head. I sure had to concentrate!

But it was an easy cloud and it stretched and dwindled real fast till it finally vanished up above the church roof, and I stood up. "That'll be ten bucks I reckon," I said.

Rufus was staring up over the church. "I can still see it," he said. "Don't you see it Harvey?" and the young feller next to him said "Clear as day, it's getting bigger if anything."

So I wasn't going to stretch out the agony and I said "Okay, you see it so you don't owe me, but I don't see it, so I guess we're quits."

He laughed and put the car into gear. "Whiteman speak with forked tongue," he said. "So long Rainmaker" and the whole wagonload of them was laughing as they drove off down the main street.

That was a good one I thought.

Jake was waiting at the hall door and he said, "Well, your on, but don't expect to be taken too serious."

I told them I'd be in touch, and I might need their help to fetch the rain in when I'd studied the situation, but what about the price?

"What do you think?" said Jake.

"Well," I said. "Seems to me you stand to make a bundle if it does rain, so why don't I cash in on that? How'd it be if each farmer gives me one tenth of what he makes? I believe that's called a tithe."

One young rancher – there was a surprising number of young people there – he said there was more to it than getting rain. A hail storm could wipe everything out.

"You got crop insurance don't you?" I said.

And Jake said "Now, you got to understand that insurance just pays the seed-money back, it don't give you no profit."

"Well," I said, "seems like farmings one big gamble, so I'll gamble too. I'll settle for one tenth of each of your profits, so if it works out we'll all be flying." Had a feeling as I said that that I might regret it, and I did I suppose, but at that stage of the game it wasn't the thing most on my mind.

So the meeting broke up, pretty good humoured too, and Jake brought the pickup round. A nice honest vehicle with a friendly kind of face and a step-up box and a long wobbly gear shift on the floor. Always did like Cornbinders. Faded blue. Radio didn't work which was fine with me, neither did any of the gauges, but Jake said there was better than a half tank of gas in her, so off I went.

That valley, if you could call it a valley when there was only one side of it had any real hills, well that valley just grew on me as I drove round the concession roads. I told myself something was unfolding for me, that there was a shape to it, not to analyse too much. And about dinnertime I drove down where there was a line of cottonwoods and a little dried up crick and I lay down by the truck and pulled a blanket over me and I was *happy*.

The weave of that blanket between me and the sky and the smell like sackcloth – I was suddenly so goddam happy I figured I'd got my childhood back. Not that my childhood was what you'd call happy, sociologically speaking, but I mean the state of just staring at the world and being free of consequences. And I thought I should be able to do this anytime, and aint that life and my perverse nature maybe, that I had to set some crazy scheme in motion just to get to be free. Unless you can be free in a trap. And there's the trouble with thinking, you get self-conscious, it's that old Walt Disney pooch running off the cliff and happy as a clam till he looks down.

So I stopped that and just lay there squinting through the open weave of the blanket, half-drowsy, half-alert, and I could see a hawk up there, a prairie falcon I guess, skating slow down that empty blue sky, and then someone blotted him out, standing over me.

I pulled off the blanket and there was this native kid, about four or five, staring at me with a solemn face, and beside him was a girl about fourteen, smiling.

She said "Hello Rainmaker."

"Who sent you?" I said, "Rufus Skylight?"

"No," she said, "We just came."

I gave them both a stick of gum and said no offence but I needed to be alone and would they just take off home, and at some point I called her "kid" and she said "I aint no kid, I'm 19." And I laughed and said "sure" and she went off in a huff. The little guy still hadn't said a word.

Now it's a funny thing about telling a story, but I didn't want to let on beforehand that that was Dar, because it was her of course and I know that, and whom I writing this for anyways? Just I had the feeling I shouldn't let on, for the sake of the telling, so's it would just come out the way I experienced it.

So maybe I just learned something about writing books. I'll think on it later. Only I would like to write books, when I think what reading has meant to me. You can say what you like in a book, and get it right. You can feel the people out there just waiting to listen. Not many, maybe, but *people*. In their own time and privacy and without distractions.

I miss Dar. I don't know if I could truly say that about anyone before, so in case she gets around to taking a run at this story, I'll put it here that I miss her.

I can just see her face when she sees her birthday present. It's a real cowgirl outfit in black suede, with boots to match like I seen Emmy Lou Harris in one time, and she'll love it. And look great in it.

But I have to say that Christmas fills me with dismay. It don't have no memories for me, and going round the stores with Dar, the stuff she was getting for her family – all the plastic, conveyor belt crap, all coming off TV, not a thing to get a kid's imagination going, I hated it. I was getting jittery so I left her to it, with the barbie dolls and g.i. joes and them luminous ponies and nursery computers. "Looks like all the indians are turning into cowboys," I said, but she was happy and said I was just weird, nothing phazes her, and I went off to read my Equinox magazine in the coffee shop.

And I thought

FAMINE IS STALKING THIS LAND DISGUISED
AS PLENTY

and I actually went and wrote that big on the men's washroom wall, which is a thing I've never done. When I was a kid I used to write things on the rafters in my uncle's shop, or on bits of paper that I'd hide under stones, when words like that come to me. Later, for a while, I'd write them on the inside walls of trucks when I was hitching around B.C.

Dar told me one time, when I let rip about something, cause I aint shy with her, "You should've been an old time preacher."

"Yeah, Billy Sunday, that's me," I said, and I grabbed her leg and tickled her all the way down to her ankle till she was screaming fit to die, and then all the way back up again. Dar can't stand you to touch her feet, can't stand having them looked at even. Beats me. We were getting to know the haybarn at the time – it still wasn't cold a month ago. That was a sweet time. I imagine that old Tom cat had his malevolent eye on us too.

Now there *is* a word. It's got violent in it and malingering and evil and male and I worked that out for myself. Some things a dictionary don't tell you about words.

I guess I left the straight row there, sort of lost my drift a bit. I went and had a beer and dozed off on the couch. Had the worst damn dream I ever had – that old Tom cat with his teeth locked in Darlene's neck and his claws working at her shoulders. He was killing her, she was dying but she was laughing. Not her own real laugh, neither. It's awful what dreams can do to a person. That's my main memory of Vancouver, bad dreams.

Well it's 3.30 in the morning and I'm sat here with a coffee because I woke up and couldn't sleep. Guess I've got used to having a body beside me. I let the collie in for company and I'm not sure he's ever been in the house before, but I told him in the morning I'd let him off his chain and he could take out that old Tom cat with my blessing if he was swift enough. Now he's settled down and asleep under the table. Keeps twitching and making little yapping sounds – guess dogs have dreams too.

I've got this school book half filled so I'd best aim for that straight row if I can.

So that first night down by the crick near Palliser I slept under the stars and was up at dawn which aint my style, and went exploring while the coffee was boiling up. It was mostly a runoff crick – you could see where Spring floods had cut deep here and there and in one place I was up to my shoulders between the narrow sides.

I looked up at those cottonwoods, and a couple of them were 50 footers, and I thought, they've been through drought before and they've come through. And then I realised there must be water still, under the crick bed, to keep them half ways going, and I got this idea that if I could find that water then somehow I'd be on the scent of calling the rain in. Don't ask me why because *I* didn't question it.

And that about being a water-diviner wasn't BS neither, because I can do that, it aint that unusual a gift, so I was going to cut me a Y twig when I saw this stumpy cow's horn sticking out of the bankside and I yarded it clear and thought, Goddam it's a *buffalo* skull, aint no cow, from the time of the herds. And I carried it down and poured out my coffee. Which was when Dar showed up aain.

She was alone and she'd a short skirt and fancy boots and black tights, and a shiny green blouse of some kind, and I said "Honey, you look like a 7th Street hooker."

And she looked me right in the eye and said "I done that too, for a while."

I shared my coffee with her and showed her the buffalo skull and she said "That's my name – Buffalo." "Darlene Buffalo?" I had to laugh. She was kind of cute in her city clothes, sat crosslegged under that old cottonwood. Sure could see a lot of her legs too. She said her dad was a hippy draft-dodger came up in the 60s. "I was supposed to be named Harmony if I was a girl," and she laughed, "But he took off on mom before I was born." "That's rough," I said. "Oh," she said, "I got the family. That's okay."

I told her I thought her white blood was good for her figure – she has a cute backside and it seems to me that native girls, however beautiful, is short in the ass department. Or maybe it wasn't then I told her that, but I did some time.

She got up and reached for my hand and said "I'll show you something," and we went over the crick bed and up beyond and I said, "Why don't you take your boots off?" but she wouldn't. And then we came to this big rock, in a round hollow, with some saskatoons growing around it, and when I got close I saw it had a *waist*. I mean there was this strip of it that was worn in all around and polished. Shiny. She still had a hold of my hand. "That's the buffalo rock," she said. "That's where they used to rub themselves."

"Goddam," I said. "It's all around us. It's got to come round again."

I know I got sort of excited because I was talking a streak and she was laughing and stumbling in those designer boots, hanging onto my arm as we went back to the crick.

I cut the Y branch and commenced walking the crick bed, and

the twig pulled down right away. "Water," I said. "You want to try?"

She took the stick and I stood behind her and held her hands till she got it right, but it didn't work for her. So I put my hand on the back of her neck, like I saw someone do once, and I guess it flowed through her because the stick started pulling like crazy and one side twisted out of her hand.

"It's like feeling a fish on the end of your line," she said.

"Maybe finding rain's like feeling a bird on the end of your line," I said.

"Your crazy," she said, but she was smiling up into my face and she had the most elegant collarbone. I got a thing about collar bones, and her boobs were just calling out to me. I was surely tempted, standing so close in the old crick bed and in case you don't know, the spring leaves and the wool of a cottonwood have the scent of a woman's intimacies about them.

"Honey, I got to think," I said. "I got to be alone."

Writing a story is like raising ghosts. It's got me horny just writing that, and nothing happened that time.

Not that she did leave right away. She's got her woman's instincts, has Dar, and she just went and sat down and poured some more coffee and asked me about myself.

Like what I did for the five years between 25 and 30, and I said I'd been sort of out of circulation.

"Prison?" she said.

I laughed and said no, though one or two people had prophesied that.

She said, "My brother was a junkie. Herbert. He overdosed in Calgary."

"That'll happen," I said. "Your a smart kid, Darlene." And I asked her how she got off the streets and she looked me in the face and said, "How'd you get off Junk?" "That's a better question," I said. "I believe the truth is, I just wearied of the company I was keeping." "That'll happen," she said and she stood up and handed me back my coffee mug. "I brung Herbert's body back, and I stayed, that's all. I always missed this place anyways, even if it drives me nuts."

I think that's when she left, but I know she said, "I'll be back, Rainmaker," which was the last time she called me that. I watched her walk away and I knew I had the hots for her, for sure, and that would have to work itself out in its own time.

Because something was going on inside of me and around them old cottonwoods. I could feel it, but I couldn't get a hold of it. I knew it would come if it was meant to and if I was ready for it.

Just figuring on things going around and coming around and water calling to water and the roots diving down and the branches reaching up and maybe those old buffalo spirits around the stone. Something.

I just let the collie dog out. The sky's lightening and he was whining at the door. Sure enough, the old Tom cat was there and the dog lit out after him and damn near got him too. Last I seen of the Tom he was glaring at me from the top of the horse-gate. I know it was me he had his eye on, not the dog. Mouth drawn back. I'll have to watch out for him.

So I wonder if all writers keep these crazy hours, or if it's just Dar not being here and me with time on my hands. Maybe I'd never write anything with her in the house. I went for that ride on Snooze and the dog come along, and we put up a Jack Rabbit and raced it to the back 40. I didn't fall off, though my thigh muscles are just whipping me. Then I slept on the couch and after that I soaked in the tub and cooked up some beans.

Now it's three in the afternoon. Seems to me that books kind of live in their own time zone eh. Makes you speculate on how a person who was writing stories could ever fit in a regular job.

I looked in at the girl's room just now, I believe Dorrie Sprintz said she was fourteen, with the computer on her desk and the correspondence course books, and I wonder what she's learning. Like, I don't see how *anyone* learns anything in school – you only learn things your ready for, and I don't think teachers have any notion how fogged out from caring most kids are. They're listening through the fog of their own concerns.

As far as I'm concerned Joannie, for instance, she teaches and she's nothing but a baby sitter, and in her case the babies are lucky cause I know Joannie and she is one what you'd call civilising influence. But the stuff there is to learn, I reckon don't get learnt till a person's long past school age.

Maybe I'm out of line, but I've got a hunch that canning the school's altogether would do just fine for us. Like Joannie's always saying we're a sub-literate culture, that or post-literate. Can the schools, and let the ones who want learning find it for themselves.

The rest can get on as usual with their TVs and credulity. We all got our systems, and once you start, there's a chain reaction. One thing leads to another. Things call out, I know that for a fact.

I believe there's a kind of map of what your meant to learn and what your meant to do with it. Like I said, one thing leads to another, it's like a family tree, and once your off and running then education is what you could call self-generating.

I know where it all started for me too, the chain reaction. I could tell you the day and the hour it started for me. Like, there I was at 15, like Johnny Prine says "muscles in his brain aint never been used," nothing in my mind except baseball and fishing and cars and just beginning to concentrate on pussy. Which wasn't doing me any good, cause to quote Mr Prine again, "There were spaces between me and whatever I said." But this 27th of August I got to go to the Rex theatre with Laura Carwithen who was supposed to let you feel her up.

I can smell that place now, and hear the sound of our feet down the sloped wood floor in the shadows. We had our popcorn finished before the Loony Tunes were done, and Laura right away untied her pony tail and there was her hair all down around her cheeks onto her shoulders, and her eyes gone all mooney and moving towards me. Hadn't occurred to me what I was getting into. But then the movie commenced, "The Yearling" it was called, with Gregory Peck, but we hadn't paid much heed to the poster outside cause seeing the film wasn't exactly the point. Except I couldn't keep my eyes off it.

It was about this piss poor family in the American south and the boy gets a pet deer named Flag on account of its tail, and times are bad and the Father's sick and the deer gets into the garden and his Mom shoots it from off the porch, and the kid runs after it with one of its legs broke and flapping and has to finish it off.

My hand was halfway down the front of Laura's blouse, cause she put it there, but it didn't get no further cause I was into the film and she was too, and I started blubbing, and she was blubbing too only it was alright for her. And when it was finished, I sat there staring at the credits, trying to get my eyes dry before the lights come on, and I saw it was made out of a book.

Afterwards we walked back towards her place and I took hold of her hand but she pulled it away and turned and said to me, "Your dumb. Your just a kid and your dumb, that's all," and she walked

off from me. She sounded pretty mad but she never told no one, and
God bless Laura Carwithen whatever fate may have befallen her.

But that was the first book I ever bought, and it cost me three
bucks which took some arriving at, and I nearly finished my
reading career right there. Cause it was a hundred times better
than the film but it was a thousand times more difficult. But it was
the start.

And I went on. Just stuff mentioned in the book your reading
leads you to another. And there's accidents too. I happened on
William Faulkner in a book called "Great Hunting Stories" that a
feller had in the Kitwanga bunkhouse. Part of a story called "The
Bear," and he's way beyond me still, and sometimes I laugh
because he seems to go on like Dar says I do, and I'm not too sure
that he always keeps to Joannie's straight row, but I know he's the
goods.

Like, cause I'm crazy about the natural world and I buy every
Equinox magazine that comes out and they have reviews of books,
which got me onto Annie Dillard and Loren Eisely, and those
people can *write*. Ms Dillard would get a real charge out of that old
Tom cat in the barn, I reckon! And that Loren Eisely – we all live in
rat country, he says. He makes what you call a metaphor for the
human mind out of a Pack Rat town.

But they're Americans. And it strikes me they talk about *pain*
so much, like they deal in pain and sorrow, same as the blues, I
guess, or Hank Williams for that matter. Like they stretch out
their pain and they elevate it. It's the U.S. way.

Seems to me, south of the border, black or white that's how they
handle tribulation. But up here, brown or white, we do it different.
We tell the story. And I never heard a yarn yet that didn't leave you
with a smile – if only for the satisfaction of having it well told.

Because, as I see it, when you tell the story the me becomes
someone else. That's what I realise now, looking back at some of
what I been writing here – when I get away from the story maybe
it's out of line, but when the story gets away from me it dont seem
too bad.

So I guess a writer of books, he has to hoe the straight row off
the bat. Either that or do like I've done and then go back and weed
it out. Makes me dizzy just to think of the work involved.

Because how do I get back to the story now? Well, I believe signs
come at you from the real world to point you at the story. And

vicey-versa I wouldn't doubt. That Jack rabbit we chased this morning put me in mind of the two Jack rabbits that started the idea for the rain.

I was laid down again under my blanket, and trying to let the notions come to me. I was just dozing really, and when I turned over and stuck my head out there was these two rabbits going at it across the crick. A full grown Jack rabbit's the size of a dog, so it was a busy and impressive sight, and when he was done he let out this scream and threw himself off her backwards, like arching himself back against the skyline, and he fell flat on his side and lay twitching. And it came to me "die for Life," cause he'd lost it, that old buck, anyone could have picked him off just then and I remembered Birdie Daniel who was Metis, saying that the french word for it was the small death. And I thought, there's next years' seed safely sown. Then the Buck rabbit recovered himself and they both loped off in separate directions.

That's when it came to me. I had this damned idea starting up and I knew I shouldn't think it through or it'd go dead on me, but it was harder'n hell to push it away, and I knew it was time to call a meeting in town right now. And so much for my dream of lounging by the crick for three weeks and being Huck Finn.

I drove the Cornbinder into town, to Jake Merrilees' house and asked would he call a meeting for the next afternoon. Everyone to be there. He said he would and I drove back to the crick, all which put some miles on the pickup that I failed to take into account later on.

When I stood up in front of those folks the next day I still didn't have it quite straight, in fact the words spilled out very simple, and I couldn't quite believe I was going to get away with it.

I told them I did believe I could bring rain to the valley and that I was going to need their help. And I said it was just a matter of concentration, and if we could all concentrate together at one time we could make it happen.

"The rain's just waiting to come round," I said. "Never you mind them satellite photographs. And the earth is just waiting to receive it."

"So what do we concentrate on?" says Jake.

"You think about rain," I said, "but you concentrate on each other." And I took a breath, but I could feel I was *on*. "I'm asking you all to make love tomorrow afternoon at 5 o'clock."

Then I waited to see if I was out of line. And then some young feller let out a great whoop of laughter and I knew I was home free, and that's how I played it from there on in.

"You mean be actually *doing* it at five o'clock."

"Uh huh."

"You chauvinist," yelled one gal, and I loved her for that, it cracked everyone up, "what about foreplay?"

"Oh I aint against foreplay by no means ma'am," I said. "You can start your preliminaries at 2 pm if you like. Just be there at 5.00."

So someone wanted to know what they'd do with the kids and "Throw a pound of green jelly beans out on the lawn," hollered someone else, and buddy next to him said, "They'd have to be brown jelly beans – aint no green grass around here."

Then this old rancher stood up and said, "Maybe Dolly and me should have the kids over to our place. I'm past all that sex stuff."

And I come back,"Any man who stands up in public and says he's past it, you know damn well he's lying to you." And they all cheered him, and he did a little dance, and his old lady covered her face in shame and delight.

So that's how it was. And at 4.30 next day I was stood by the cottonwoods looking at the pitiless empty sky and wishing it could be true, but really beginning to wonder where I should head for next.

Which is when Dar showed up. Just in jeans and a shirt this time.

"I wouldn't want you to be left out of the act," she said.

"No," I said. "No, no, this aint the time." She kept walking towards me with a sweet and wicked smile. "Look here," I said. "I appreciate this, and you are as tempting as they come, but I got work to do. A person can't get distracted when he's keeping a promise to himself."

She came right on, with slow, easy steps. Came right up against me and grabbed my jeans at the pockets and give me what we used to call a snuggie when we were kids.

"I'll help you," she said.

"Dammit no," I said but I guess I didn't back off enough. Her eyes were that dark and pretty and calling me down to her.

"Hell Darlene," I said, "you know the old indian chiefs and medicine men wouldn't touch a woman when there was healing or fighting to be done. Have some respect, eh."

She just laughed and kissed me on the nose. She was that sure of herself.

"Listen," I said, "between you and me this is all a crock of shit what I've got them doing, but I aim to give it a shot. I got to concentrate."

"It's near five o'clock," she said. "You'n me might make all the difference."

And then we were kissing and anything but would have gone altogether against nature.

Mind you, I'm oldfashioned enough to think when a girl steps out of her pants before you even got your hand on her shirt buttons, she's way ahead of the game, but she'd got me going and that's all there was to it.

I went and dragged the blanket over by the trees and took my shirt off and lay down with her. The sun moved over a bit and started flashing and flickering through them dry, whispery cottonwood leaves and we commenced the game.

So there I was with my pants round my ankles, sprawled out in the daylight, me and a juicy young girl, dogging it by that old crick bed and me supposed to be calling down rain.

It seemed wrong, or maybe I just got distracted by my mind and I kind of fell out of step with her. I just needed to be still. All the same, I know she could see the laugh beginning to tug at my mouth, thinking about all the citizens in the valley right now making time together. Cause however much I wanted there to be something in my rain idea, following the treadmill back and bringing the raintime round again, it suddenly began to seem awful funny. Like it did when I brought the notion up at the meeting. Maybe you don't have to be solemn to get serious things done.

Dar wasn't complaining, though she was watching me and I guess she was wondering, and she kept making little sounds and pulling at my back ribs.

Then I saw these two dragonflies in the air above one of the tree roots. What my auntie used to call devil's darning needles only those were electric blue and these were pink. Sort of neon pink and they were doing it. I don't know how they manage it, cause the one on top he sort of twists his tail out and round and down and then up into hers, and they make this sort of heart shape and how they keep aloft at the same time I do not know.

And I said, "Look at that now, it aint just people who're in on the act!" And she tipped her head back to look and that lifted her closer against me and then we were doing it, oh my god were we doing it. Dar started laughing, laughing and crying out, "Piper, Piper" all together, and I was kissing her under her ear and our bodies were doing their own dance together. I reached out to that old tree root to pull us closer, if that was possible, and my eyes come open and *her* eyes were eating me up, she'd done laughing now, and the sky over us had turned her brown eyes blue-glazed, like a head-shot deer's and off I went with her – I could see the long white tracers of myself bursting out into the blue sky of her eyes. I swear.

We were still for a while and then she said, real quiet, "Heavenly days, Piper – I'm in my glory." Which grew to be a catch phrase with us.

And me, well I guess a person can never trust his recollections in that department, but it seemed to me then, and it still does, that I'd been waiting thirty four years to find a lover like that. "Oh God," I said, that was all I *could* say. I was as emptied out as the old Jack rabbit the day before. Lost to the world, we both were. Which means we dozed off of course, till I came to with a start. "Honey," I said, "we had our fun, but I got to get moving," and I grabbed my shirt.

I couldn't tell how long we'd been laying there, the sun had moved over some and the wind had picked up a bit in the leaves, but it didn't seem all that much time had gone by. "Come on," I said. "I need the blanket."

Being as she was still bare-assed naked from the waist down it was a tad hard to concentrate. Dar has skin like coffee cream.

"Where you going?" she said.

"I planned on taking the truck to the next town," I said. "I'll leave word for Jake Merrilees where it's at."

"I'll come with you," she said and got up off the blanket.

I said, "Alright, you can drive the truck back in." But she knew and I knew that wasn't how it would be. Besides it turned out later that she didn't know how to drive then!

"And you can navigate too," I said. "You know these back roads and I'd sooner not run into anyone."

She knew the roads alright, but the pickup sent up so much dust you could have seen from ten miles off the route we took. And that wind was a fair bit stronger now, and it was blowing the dust around. It was a mean dry wind that would shrivel your sinuses in a minute. And I started feeling bad, seeing that dust getting up, cause half the fence lines in that valley is on ten foot piles of old top soil blown off in the Dirty Thirties.

Dar laid her head on my knee and started fiddling with the radio knobs, and I told her forget it, but just then we hit a patch of washboard and my head near went through the cab roof, and in came the radio loud and clear – "Didn't know God loves honky tonk angels," I had to laugh.

But right then the engine coughed and dickered and died on me, so I brought her down a gear and gunned it but she only caught for a couple seconds and died again. Which meant only one thing – no gas.

I swatted the wheel and pushed Dar away from my knee. "Godammit," I said, "you brought me bad luck." Which is the only mean thing I have ever said to Dar.

"It's not the end of the world," she said, and she surely gave me the look.

"Yeah, I'm sorry," I said, "but here we could be stuck all night."

She said not to worry, Rufus Skylight and his brother came through this way every day about seven. "This is Indian Territory your in," she said.

The radio was still going, and Dar stretched out again like a cat on the seat and commenced playing with my leg and tickling my ribs inside my shirt, but I couldn't relax, I was what they call uptight alright.

Even when she kneeled up and got to nibbling my ear and making ho-ho noises and running her tongue around it.

Then she stopped and said, "You aint going to believe this, Piper."

But I seen it already, in the left wing mirror. A long white cloud was spilling down the hillsides, like a glacier busted loose.

It was wide as it was long and it was coming fast, hugging the earth, sliding into the valley behind us.

We were stuck for sure now. Whether that cloud was good for forty days of rain or a couple hours, this road and all of the concessions would be gumbo soon as it hit. It would be a long dirty walk out for us but I couldn't get the grin off my face and Dar was just screaming with laughter and all over me.

We got to yelling and whooping and it was growing dark behind us, the air turned almost purple, and when the rain hit it was like bird shot on the cab roof and mud was splashing up on the glass inside a minute.

We were singing along with the radio, "Out with the truckers and the kickers and the cowboy angels" and "Long may you run", it was a good station, and "On the road again" and it was like we were under water.

I was what you'd call elated. "My stars, Dar," I said. "Aint nothing can louse us up now excepting hailstones or hoppers."

Which is when the rain quit. Didn't peter out or nothing, just quit, and the sun came back, shining in on us, and when I got out and stood on the running board all I could hear was water running and bubbling and settling, but what I saw was that cloud heading out away from us towards the open prairie like it had jet engines slung on it.

I stared after it and I could see it thinning out and breaking into streaks, still going like hell, and then you could see the sky through it in places, hard and blue, and before that raincloud was halfways to the horizon it was just gone. Vanished away.

And the road and the fields were steaming already.

Dar was out the other side of the truck, prancing around in the mud, her legs streaked all red and brown and black, only time I believe I ever did see her minus her boots or shoes. I went around to her and we commenced this goofy hoe-down dance, and I began singing, high in my nose, "Raining violets," "and if it's raining, don't have no regrets," strutting like Al Jolson, trying to keep upright in that gumbo. "What's that supposed to be?" she said, and I told her Al Jolson was this Jewish American made himself a million impersonating a black man, and she said that was the dumbest thing she ever heard in her life.

And then we both, in the self same minute, thought about the folks in Palliser, bare assed on their porches, looking at what they just brought to pass. And we got near hysterical.

Rufus and Harvey did come by a little later, and the way things went after that was, there was prairie crocus and shoots of wheat four inches tall by the week's end, and the valley turned green, only the hopper eggs got started just as fast and by mid June there wasn't much to see in that territory excepting hungry insects.

And I suppose the hail didn't trouble coming round this summer, since there was nothing left to spoil.

Which only goes to show, I guess, but exactly what I couldn't say.

But I have what I believe is referred to as Writer's Cramp in my fingers and my left shoulder. And I feel near as cleaned out as the old Jack rabbit. I believe I'll get a beer and soak in the tub awhile

and then put on the TV. There's been no music or TV in the house
since I've been alone here.

The Flames are hosting the Red Wings and they'll be on in about
a half hour.

Anyways, I did get the Cornbinder out of it, and the name for
being a good loser, and Dar and me are doing fine so far. If it hasn't
rained every afternoon since, it aint been for lack of trying.

So, like the feller said, that's all she wrote.

> The cards aint marked
> The deck aint stacked
> Your hands aint tied
> Your bags aint packed

WE TALK OF DROUGHT WHILE THE FLOOD
BREAKS OVER US

Alex

FOR GEORGE YEMEC

ALEX STANDS BY HIS FRONT STEPS, watching the lawn. He holds the sprinkler delicately in his brutalised hands and plans where to set it down first. His neighbour comes out to get mail from the box on his porch and calls cheerily. "Lawn's looking good there!" Alex barely catches the words, but his flat, usually sullen features crease into a grin; he spreads his arms in clumsy pantomime and "Good!" he barks, "New springler!"

His neighbour understands Alex's deafness and he shouts with the brisk cheerfulness that seems never to leave him. They talk about the drought and the heat, but his neighbour speaks too rapidly for Alex to follow him clearly. They talk about the new house going up across the street, on the half lot that was a garden just a month ago, and as Alex starts to grumble about the way things are built now, his neighbour is already scanning one of his letters. "Well," he says, "someone's making a buck anyway," and he laughs, bounding back up the steps and through his front door. Alex recovers himself.

He turns the red plastic dial where the hose connects to the sprinkler, sets the device down gently at the south east corner of the tiny lawn, and goes back down the side of the house to turn on the faucet.

When the water has squirmed its way through the hose the sprinkler jets out in an oval pattern, rises and then tilts slowly back across the grass. Alex is pleased with himself for mastering it without the help of the box-instructions. He stands with his arms folded, watching.

The front yard is his territory and pride. The back lawn fills him with rage and shames him in his neighbour's eyes. All summer, through the vacations, his children lie there, sunbathing, playing

107

the radio, anointing their young bodies with suntan oil. The oil eats at the grass – the back lawn is blotched with khaki islands, a map of his children's indolence. They can lie there for hours, doing absolutely nothing, getting up only to fetch drinks from the fridge, or to lean on the roofs of their friends' cars and talk and laugh.

Once Alex came round the side of the house and found his neighbour at the fence, asking the children to turn down their radio. Instead of defending them for the noise he could scarcely hear, Alex turned on them, incensed by their insolent, lazy response, roaring that they were pigs and lazy fools and bad neighbours, and then, at the corner of his eye, he saw his neighbour shrugging and winking in conspiracy with Stefan. Brought short, Alex growled something at the dog and stumped into the house.

Methodically, for there is all the time in the world and when he retires next year there will be too much time, Alex goes back to the faucet, turns it off and comes back to reposition the sprinkler. He does not hear much these days, thirty years in the factory have dulled him to all but the loudest sounds, but yesterday, while the boys lobbed a frisbee in the street, some young workmen started putting up siding on the new house, and as Alex was crossing the lawn a staple-gun went off – *K'iu, K'iu, K'iu* – and he threw himself down on his face. The boys were laughing, so were the workmen, as that machine pistol racket went on, so close, and he clambered up, unsure if they'd seen him, and then in fury flung down the old sprinkler and broke it.

He had to walk into town to buy a new one, stalking out through the back where Katja lay, absorbed by herself in the sun, and off through the lanes. Alex always walks through the back lanes, past the garages, the garbage cans, the kids playing hockey or basketball, where the cats prowl and fight and glare down from fence posts and garbage-lockers. It may be because of the silence and privacy. Perhaps, though it would never occur to him, there is a reminiscence here, under the wide sky, of his childhood village. Except, of course, for the cars parked everywhere.

He walked down to the hardware store by the Safeway, five blocks away, but when he couldn't see what he needed he had to point and use dumbshow, because the word for sprinkler had slipped away from him, and then he could not understand what the boy at the store was saying, and he walked out, sure that the blood was going to burst in his temples, and went all the way down town till he saw one displayed in a shop window.

His lawn is perfect. It is the only one on the street without a single scar, a single unevenness, a single dandelion or daisy. The sprinkler is at the north east corner now, playing its fan of water-arches back towards the house. Next week the city will start rationing, but Marika will save the dishwater for him. He nods in satisfaction – the new sprinkler takes its time, it does a better job than the old one.

A white car comes down the street, much too fast; even he can hear the clashing pulse of the music playing inside it. It turns without stopping at the sign, and heads the wrong way down the one-way street. It will be parking in his lane now, some friend of Stefan's or Gregor's. Soon they'll be sauntering out, ignoring him, to throw the frisbee around, or to demand the hose to spray themselves down. Let them wait.

He should rejoice in his children's grace and freedom, but it affronts him. He has a grievance against the young. On his fiftieth birthday he challenged a smirking apprentice to carry a grader blade with him across the shop floor. They had gone twenty feet when the boy dropped his end of the massive plate, it twisted in Alex's hands and smashed into both of his knees. He was in hospital for five months, on crutches for almost a year, and when he went back to the factory they'd shifted him into Maintenance. His knees will not bend now, they ache when the wind blows from the south, they wake him some nights, clenching between the muscles in his calves and his thighs, so that he bites his lip and drenches the sheets with the stink of pain.

Since Katja was six, the children have spoken English together, and Marika went along with that. She even uses the English names that their friends know them by – Steve and Greg and Jay. They answer him in English even when he makes a point of being jocular in the old tongue – they understand it perfectly well but they will not speak it except when they visit Marika's mother. He has not learned enough English to understand all their replies, or to be sure when they are mocking him. He doesn't realise, either, that he shouts whenever he talks to them. Sometimes Marika laughs with them, and he clenches his hands and scowls at the table until they have left.

Hardly ever now do they eat together – the children have money to eat out, to order in pizzas, to eat when they feel like it, on the run, though they do precious little work. Evening jobs, packing at Safeway on Saturday afternoon, delivering groceries, for the boys

have their drivers' licences now. And Katja works three evenings
at some restaurant. And they contribute nothing to the home, or if
they do it goes to Marika.

Ten feet above Alex's head a Mourning Dove hugs herself onto
the eggs in her flimsy nest. The Silver Fir is the only tree in the
front yard; it seems scarcely to have grown since they bought the
house twelve years ago. Alex does not hear the endless throb of the
mate's call from the telegraph pole at the corner, but he has a
feeling for the doves. They're the only birds except sparrows and
starlings and pigeons, half-tame things, which endure the fierce
prairie winters, and from Christmas on he puts out bird seed on his
steps for them, and wages war on the alley cats.

His ally in that war is Snoopy, the beagle which Marika bought
for Katja's thirteenth birthday. Sometimes he feels it's as close as
he comes to having a friend, though he hates its name and will only
call it *Pess*. Katja soon tired of it and he makes it an excuse for his
walks through the back lanes, treats it with a crude tenderness,
abusing it fondly, tugging its ears till it yelps a little, though not
out of real pain or fear. Yet though it is grateful for the attention, it
is not a real friend – it will always choose Marika if she wants it,
and it goes rushing and skidding and yelping down the hardwood
hallway if any of the children call it by name. He feels that they do
it to take the dog away from him, for as soon as it's found them they
lose interest.

Alex goes back to the faucet and yells for the dog, and when it
comes trotting round the house he demands that someone fetch
him the leash. But no one responds. He growls disgustedly and
goes round the back. Katja is lying on her back in a skimpy blue
bikini, Gregor stands in his shorts by the back gate, talking to the
boys with the white car. They all ignore him. He gets the leash
from the porch, grumbling indistinctly at Marika who is ironing
something of Katja's in the kitchen. When he goes out he barks at
his daughter "Why don't you do anything for yourself? You think
your mother's a slave?" The boys look up at the sound of the old
tongue, and grin. Katja yawns and sits up, reaching for the tube of
tanning lotion on the ruined grass.

Next door the neighbour and his wife are sitting with two
friends, drinking beer on the back steps. They wave and call. He
sees one of their friends has his eyes on Katja, they are talking
about the girl. His neighbour looks at her too, with mingled
amusement and lust.

Alex forces the dog to sit while he clips on the leash, then he goes to move the sprinkler across by the fir tree, comes back to turn on the water, and after a minute's contemplation leaves by the front gate, and walks slowly down to the corner.

No one is working on the new house across the street today, but he can scarcely believe it has risen so quickly. All the prefabricated struts and panels, all the equipment and short-cut devices. Marika said it was selling for $70,000. Twelve years ago his house cost him $12,000, all paid for now, and at first he was happy there; he'd done well for an immigrant, he'd achieved what a *kulak's* son should dream of doing. The backyard that is now his disgrace was a vegetable garden, but his knees would not bend, and when Marika took the hospital job they put in a lawn, and then the children began to change.

He crosses from the corner into the backlane by the store that the Greeks have bought, and goes slowly down towards the park and the embankment. In the last two weeks the creek has shrunk to a foul-smelling ooze. Alex does not notice much around him, he pays little heed to the dog except when it skirmishes with a fat terrier behind a new villa and then he yanks it clear of the ground by its leash and aims a kick at the yapping adversary.

There are couples on the embankment – teenagers talking, smoking, lying under the willows in each other's arms. He's as invisible to them as he is to the kids who play hockey in the lanes. They look right through him – no one talks to anyone, no one smiles, no one shows any respect. Single or in couples, they're as separate from each other as the neighbours on his street. It's as though everyone here just passes through, like fantastically rich gypsies.

Alex lets the dog off the leash and waits for the aching to leave his knees. The teenagers! Last October he could not get back to sleep and when he got out of bed he saw a car parked by the back gate with its engine running. He knew it was Katja, Marika said children today all stayed out late, they must not make Katja an outcast. And he guessed what was up, and got dressed, and went out through the yard. He was ready to haul out some young punk kissing and pawing at his daughter, but what he'd seen through the steamed-up windshield was Katja kneeling up on the seat, all over the boy. She had his shirt undone, and Alex had seen the back of her thighs in those green tights where her skirt was hiked up, and he'd gone back to the house.

She isn't close to being a woman, no hips to speak of, breasts like apples, she's *lean*, like the girls on the billboards, on TV, in the magazines, who stare back at you. And she behaves like that, as often as not in her brothers' company, with those bite-marks on her neck that she doesn't bother to hide.

Stefan is filling out, he looks at last as if he may become a real man, and he's nearly a foot taller than Alex. For that matter, all of the children are taller than their father. Last week Stefan bought a Chevrolet and Alex couldn't help but be impressed by that, thinking of himself at that age, and Stefan only just finished school. But after he went out to admire it, nodding proudly to his watching neighbour, he found himself left out and then, when they had the hood up and were trying to get it to run more smoothly, and he pushed through and tapped the round pan on top and said, "This must come off, you must clean the insides" – because he had seen them do that at the factory – Stefan had laughed and said something he could not catch to the boy he'd driven up with. And the boy was the one who had been with Katja in the car that night. Alex felt the blood push into his face and he stalked back, under his neighbour's eyes, to the front of the house.

By the time Alex was nineteen he had grown used to the touch and smell of death, to the eyes that stared back at you. He had seen his brother Stefan struck by an explosive bullet from a machine-pistol and had wiped the snot-like brain debris off his own cheek. He had seen men who'd lain numb and dying for ten minutes suddenly writhe up on their knees and scream and flail madly as the last pains broke through the nerves of their shocked flesh. He had seen snow on fire, he had seen children burning. He had fired at men, armed and unarmed, and hit them. He had cut the throats of two bolshevik officers, held at gunpoint against a tamarack tree. He had starved and chewed the loam under forest leaves. He had watched the women and daughters raped in houses where men lay dead in the next room. And after that, and two prison camps with typhus and dysentry, he had come to Canada and worked in the open phosphate mine on a prairie so much like home, and then he'd found work in the factory, making harvesters and bulldozers for the huge new farms and the straight, straight roads that went nowhere.

The bolsheviks took his father, his childhood, his country, but what can he do with the hatred he's learning now – for the careless good fortune he has worked to provide his children with? Helplessly, each year, he has seen the money he makes go on the gadgets and toys that the world had not dreamed of when he came here.

He growls at the dog to come to him and sits on a bench, staring down at the shrunken creek. There are shopping carts and bicycle wheels sticking out of the mud, tatters of plastic bags cling to exposed muskrat dens. It is hard for Alex to think about making love, to turn to Marika without thinking of violent things. Sometimes his rage is transformed in the darkness and he grabs for her, pushing her thighs apart, thrusting himself quick and heavy upon her and against the stabs of his ruined knees. She is heavy and slack, yet this is what a real woman's body should be, as his is a real man's body. Sometimes he looks at Katja and wishes on her the revenge of a woman's body, for he thinks that must be what she dreads most. Whenever he passes a pretty girl in the back lanes he scowls ferociously out of shyness, and sometimes he finds himself turning to watch as she walks away.

Marika has friends. Three days and two evenings she works at the hospital and she's busy at the social club. But Alex will only go with her, these days, to the Easter reunion. Yet he is the only one who goes to church, though he goes as a reproof, for at his age, after the years of work and providing, it is he who should stay at home and they who should stand for the family before the icons and the congregation.

She still does everything a good Ukrainian wife should, but she does it with a challenge, with a cool air as if there were an audience, and it has all lost its savour for him. And often he imagines striking out at her, but even if she guessed it, she knows he will not, as he has not struck the children since they left grade school, for he told her before they were married about his mother's wrecked eye and her deafness on one side, and how his father took the strap to him and his brother Stefan in the yard, in freezing December, and cut them almost to the bone, and he'd said he would never see that done in his family, that those ways had been left behind, but now sometimes he envies his father's certainty and sense of himself before the Russians took everything, and often he feels that his father was right. But this is the New World, with nothing to replace the old ways but luxuries; where the years of a man's labour come to ashes and boredom and neglect.

Alex is thinking about his lawn, soaking up the good water before the restrictions come in. And then he remembers his half-promise to go with Marika tonight to the social club, for her brother is coming to town. He should just have said *No* flat out, for he will not go. He bends to clip the leash back on the dog's collar and eases himself to his feet. As he heads back towards the houses he rehearses grievances to himself to justify breaking his promise.

He's beginning to hate the Community. It is partly his deafness and his stubborn neglect of it, his refusal to use the mail-order hearing-aid that Marika gave him two Christmases back, so that he cannot hear half of what they say; but he despises their contentment, their easy gestures and slogans and nostalgia. He knows it's mostly lies, all pretenses, yet they are his tribe. But Mitra Berov, with his tearful anthem-singing, *Monotonously Rings the Little Bell*, etcetera, things he learned in Canada from records, and his launching into those Cossack dances in the middle of every party; Berov who owns a Ford dealership now and has, they say, a heart of flint. All in their UPA uniform tunics. Alex was never issued a uniform, and he takes no pride in the medals he won and was never given, though he could order them from Winnipeg. They lost the war.

Alex has a sudden image of Katja, a few months old, held against his shoulder on the couch in their old apartment. Her wet lips and her tiny flawless hands, while Stefan jounced on his knee and played *tarpan* and roared like a warrior. The ways of the memory are inexplicable, and Alex strives all he can to live squarely with what is real. He lets the dog lead him back through their usual lanes.

The worst is Bryllo, "The Colonel", who works in a bank, a merchant's son like most of the well-off immigrants, who always tries to flatter Alex by saying he knew about his "outfit," heard wonderful things about their "work." How could he have heard of them? That man takes more pride in his white marshall's beard than anything else – stretching his tunic more each year, his eyes getting more and more pig-like each time Alex sees him. His hands look, and feel, like bread. And the worst of it is that his wife and children treat him like a hero. "The Colonel" – Alex remembers no titles except *chief* and *kid*. All that talk and lies and boasting – what is there to boast about? There is no no one to give honour to losers. Why should there be?

Alex stops at the street corner while the dog lifts its leg at the stop sign. Bryllo should be careful, he thinks – that mouth of his could get him into trouble. The wheels keep turning – he could find himself on trial for war crimes one of these days.

The paper will be there when he reaches home. It's his only shared pleasure of the day. Marika reads it to him, translating where necessary, as he drinks cup after cup of sweet tea and cross-examines her, demands that she re-read things. He's as addicted to the Police Report as she is to her soap operas. Every day now there seem to be muggings. Groups of youngsters cornering old men, snatching ladies' purses, beating up people in parking lots and back streets. They never get caught. During the evening Alex plays over the incidents in his mind, fleshing out the reports, sensing the hoodlums invisibly taking charge of the city, preparing for them.

Stefan's blue Chevrolet is parked by the front gate, engine running, and Marika is getting into the back. Stefan yells out of the window "Come on, Dad, I'll take you for a ride." The dog whines and drags at the lead. "Where you go?" roars Alex, suspicion on his face. "Just up the highway a few miles, see how she goes." Marika leans towards the open door, smiling: "Come on," she says, "come, we will go in style!"

"A moment," says Alex and takes the dog in through the gate. The lawn is so wet now that water is pooling around the trunk of the fir tree. Alex goes on to turn off the tap and sees the evening paper lying on the steps. After the drive Marika will want to get dressed up for the social and there will be no time for her to read to him. Besides, she will be angry that he is not coming. He glowers at the paper, goes slowly to the gate and climbs into the car. It revs up and moves even before he's got the door closed. He grabs a brief look at his lawn and the dog, leash trailing, with its paws on the fence top.

The boy in the passenger seat is the one who was parked with Katja last October. She has a new fellow now, a cadet from the Mountie barracks, but this boy still comes around, quite at ease. He chats to Stefan and Marika and smiles casually at Alex, turning in his seat and resting his arm on the backrest by Stefan's shoulder. Alex stares at the hand, imagines it upon Katja's flesh, and turns away. He stares woodenly out the window as the houses give way to factories and silos, and then to the open prairie.

The city ends so suddenly, there is nothing to protect it, and the wheeling grainfields are enough like the land he came from for a war to seem possible here, with famine and refugees, the mad war that breeds itself, that everyone lies about, where you can't tell one side from another. The bolsheviks whose throats he cut had been prisoners already. The SS party they'd taken them from had been mostly Ukrainian. Six years without a harvest. The land and the air can stink as badly as a dying creek.

The car tilts like a boat and overtakes a semi at crazy speed. Marika gasps and grips her seat, but Alex has scarcely noticed. "Steve," she says firmly, "you just turn right around and drive me home *slow*, you hear. I've had enough of this."

Steve laughs and pulls a screeching U-turn at the next cut-through. "Looks like Dad's out of it anyways!" he says, and turns on the radio. His friend's hand slaps the seat-back in time with the music.

Alex does go to the social, and even gets drunk a little, which is rare for him, but he goes up to bed as soon as they get home, leaving Marika to drink tea in the kitchen with her brother and his wife. As soon as he's in bed he wishes he'd stayed with them; he doesn't wish to be left out, for they're good farming people, and they'll be laughing now and telling stories in the old tongue. But he lies there in his silence, and is soon asleep.

When he was eighteen he learned that you must never sleep on your back, that you must not snore, that men who snored at night in the woods or fields ended up with their throats slit, or their companions shot around them. It was called "waking up dead."

He does not know that Marika blocks her ears against his coarse snoring, that Katja gave her some ear-plugs for her birthday, that it's his snores which cause his raw throat and palate in the mornings, that often when he gasps awake at two or three in the morning his own snoring has woken him.

He sleeps on his back beside Marika in the soft bed, and snores and dreams. It is often the same dream now.

It's late evening, in some dark part of town, behind the cathedral, but the wall is high on one side of the lane, it's something like the fort in his mother's town, there's a kind of dance music, faint, from a closed courtyard, a smell of smoke and frost in the air, and kerosene. The only lights shine feebly through shutters and at the cracks of doors.

A cat slinks past him, flattening itself against the wall, for the lane has narrowed into an alleyway, and he knows he is being followed. Two figures detached themselves form a knot of nogoods by a cafe doorway, and it is their footsteps he hears as he pauses, their cool laughter and then the whispering as another figure joins them from a gateway.

He moves on again and they follow; they do not know that it is he who is stalking them. The alley gets narrower still, the walls higher as they turn sharply to the left, with one dim gas lamp, yellowish green in a bracket above his head. There is no sound now but his breathing. He waits. Then he hears their steps again, the hiss of their clothing along the walls.

He speeds up. Now they will think he is lost and panicking, and just where the lamplight fails there's another right turn, a dead end past a doorway. The muggers come on, past him, and stop. They are trapped.

They see him, and check for a moment, off guard. Then they smile, casual and vicious. They wear always his children's faces.

He turns on them and pounds their faces into blood and hair with his huge anger, with his great man's fists, until they are nothing but obliterated stains and his fists keep on beating at the stones and crumbling mortar of the cul de sac.

The Running
of the Deer

THE AIR OUTSIDE THE CHURCH was alive and sparkling. Ice-motes swarmed, winking, around the clouds of breath on the steps, and the sidewalk and cars were aglint with hoar-frost, the bare trees furred with it. In one hour, the world had changed.

There were Van Gogh auras round the street lamps, prismatic and scintillant, but the cheerful voices on the path seemed loud and brittle and soon they were muffled by the sound of starters and engines, and the harsh shuffle of ice-scrapers.

A low cloud of exhaust slipped through the gateway, pungent and rubbery in the cold, and then there were doors slamming, more distant voices calling "Goodnight!" and "Happy Christmas!", even the double toot of a horn as one car pulled away.

The priest stood in the shelter of the porch, his cigarette smoke blue and lazy, shivering in his surplice as he shook hands and chatted perfunctorily. Skye was down on one knee, tucking Ben's scarf in and fastening the hood of his parka. "Well, Ben," the priest said cheerily, "we *are* up late, aren't we?" The shepherd of the flock, Jimmy noted, was not at ease with the young. "Quite the young man now, eh?"

The little boy stood, between importance and shyness, and Jimmy followed his grandson's eyes to the priest's hands, the black rims under three of the fingernails, and smiled at the child's prim distaste.

When Jimmy lit his own cigarette, the priest turned to him and smiled. "There are not many of us left," he said. "Last month I had to fly to Moncton; four hours without a smoke. It was purgatory!"

Jimmy laughed: "I just tell them self-righteousness is carcinogenic."

"It's all for the best, I'm sure," said the priest. "We must bear our cross. And will you be visiting long, Mr Sievewright?"

Jimmy winked at Skye as she stood up and adjusted her own scarf. "A week in the city is all I could stand."

"Now you can't call Whitby the city," the priest protested. "We have quieter values here."

"The city is gobbling you up already. I give it two years. Next time I'm down you'll be holding drive-through confessions."

"Merciful heavens!" the priest rolled his eyes and trod on his cigarette butt. "A cynic on Christmas Morning!" He turned to Skye and her husband: "So how is the little one doing?" It was Larry who answered: "She's good," he said, "We almost got a whole night's sleep last night." "What would you know about that?" Skye poked his arm, "The next one I'll bottle-feed, and you'll have to do your share!"

"The next one?" Jimmy said, "Dammit, girl, you're not just a breeding machine."

"It's tough for the old freedom-fighters," Skye told the priest. "When I was 15 I used to come home and give my father and mother hell for smoking marijuana."

The priest shook his head. "I hope to see large families coming back," he said, "The happy children in this parish are *not* from progressive families."

Jimmy flicked his cigarette out over the steps. Ben charged down to stamp on it. "You must be freezing to death, Father," Jimmy said. "Let's get going, eh Ben? C'mon, Skye."

"Grandchildren are a blessing, you'll agree?" said the priest.

Jimmy raised his hands: "I agree," he said, "I won't argue."

They said "Happy Christmas" all round and the priest huddled back into the church. They heard the deadlock snap to. The porch light went off before they were out on the sidewalk.

"God, I hate the smell of priests," Jimmy said.

"*Father*," Skye glared, and shook her head.

"It's clammy," he insisted, "stale sperm, unwashed sheets, gobbled porridge ..."

Larry snorted with laughter. Skye slipped her arm through his. Her grey suede coat was elegant, so was her newly bobbed hair, and her figure had come back amazingly, but Jimmy knew she had closed a door somewhere that could have stayed open.

"You don't change, Father," she said. "I guess you practise being outrageous in front of a mirror."

Ben had run ahead, trying to slide on the frosted sidewalk. He waited for them under a street lamp.

"But they *do* smell," said Jimmy, "they smell vile."

"What abut nuns?" said Larry.

"Who smells?" Ben demanded and Skye went "*Sssh!*" but "*Priests!*" declared Jimmy, taking his grandson's hand. Secretly, he feared *he'd* smell bad to a child; he was always careful not to breathe out near the boy's face.

Before Ben could respond, Skye said, "Don't listen to him, Ben, he just likes to aggravate," and, with some feeling, "Father, it's Christmas Morning and Ben's first Midnight Mass, and I won't *have* it!"

They walked on, past another street lamp. Ben looked up, from one to the other, trying anxiously to decode that exchange.

"It's a singular thing," Jimmy told him. "The whole time your mother was a girl, my name was Jimmy. And now, all of a sudden, she calls me 'Father'."

Skye leaned her head on Larry's shoulder, and sighed. The little boy groped through the adult tensions: "Shall *I* call you Jimmy, Grandad?" His mother smiled.

"Why not?" Jimmy said, "if it feels right. *Would* it feel right to call me Jimmy?"

"No."

Jimmy laughed out loud, his eyes merry at Skye's as he hugged Ben against his leg. "Keep that up," he said. "Don't ever say 'Yes' when you mean 'No'. For the rest of your life. Promise?"

"Okay, I promise, Grandad."

"How about 'No', when you mean 'Yes'?" Larry chimed in.

"He'll have to learn that from his mother –" and then he let go of the boy's hand, turned and "Oh Christ," he said, "that sounded as if it meant something, but it didn't. Ignore the old fart, okay?"

Ben gurgled with laughter, though his eyes checked his parents' faces. "You're funny, Grandad," he said, "You're *silly* sometimes!"

Jimmy took his hand again, "I know," he said, "It comes from living out in the woods with the wolves and the bears!"

"Oh sure, Jimmy," said Larry.

"It's true. There are three little brush wolves down in the swamp, I see their tracks most mornings. Got within twenty yards of them last week." He squeezed Ben's hand: "They're just little wolves," he said, "no danger to anyone."

"What about the bears, Grandad?" The boy's eyes were big.

"Well I see one or two every Fall, gorging themselves on berries."

"Would they eat you?"

"No, they stay out of people's way. They're only dangerous if you get between them and their cubs."

Ben walked on quietly for a minute and then slipped his hand loose and ran ahead. He was singing scraps of carols from the service: "*The rising of the sun and The running of the deer And the playing of the merry organ Sweet singing in the choir.*" He was skipping, on his second wind after nearly falling asleep during communion, kicking up the light covering of snow. For they had left the suburban streets now – across the road were still open fields, though a purple billboard, with antique scroll lettering, announced:

MAPLE ACRES
prime residential development
FROM $97,000
a few units still available
enquire at on site office

and humped like sleeping dinosaurs in the field were earth-moving devices and bales of white drainage tile.

The street lamps were less frequent now, but they and the half-moon bounced enough light off the snow to make everything clear. There were other signs across the road, one announced a shopping plaza for the following year, another an industrial park: "WILL BUILD TO SUIT."

Skye and Larry walked arm in arm, talking softly. Jimmy stayed a few yards in front of them, with his eye on Ben, up ahead. Walking on paved sidewalk brought his age home to him; he thought of himself as fit, and gauged that by his breathing and his ability still to climb over beaver-felled poplars, to push through the cedar-brush, to chop and carry firewood. But here it was all level and hard, and he felt suddenly skeletal – as if he were throwing his legs out, one at a time in front of him, and it was the weight of his boots that dragged them to their destination.

There was the unmistakable honking of geese, to their left, and he turned to see a skein of twenty or thirty birds, flying low over the houses. "What in hell are geese doing around this time of year?" he said. "They're here all the year round," Skye told him. "We hear them every night." "It's crazy," he said, "they're supposed to fly South. *My* geese left a month ago." "People feed them, I guess," said Larry, "and there's open water year round by the power station, and the edge of the lake." "God damn," he growled. "It's all upside down." "Yes, dear," Skye purred, her shorthand for *don't rant, don't fuss, don't give lectures.*

"I should be ashamed for having brought you into this lousy world," he said defiantly.

"Shame's not your strong suit, dear." And he heard Larry snigger.

He'd better keep quiet – he'd get petulant, and fierce, and get caught in the wrong and ... Besides, he was as bad as she was.

No one could get under his skin like Skye could. The air swarmed with irritants whenever they got together. She was worse than her mother; in fact relationships with your children could be just like wasted marriages. You knew exactly how to taunt, or deflate, or evade; and you never gave credit for change, for learning new things. The only change they'd see in each other would be physical. It was murder.

God preserve him from a stroke, and his daughter's caretaking. So long as he had his wits, and the strength to pull the trigger.

Yes, he did feel skeletal. His thick coat and the layer of scarves and sweaters, the long Stanfields, were like the hide of an old bear at the end of a long, long winter.

Maybe she *did* hold resentments still. Wasn't it enough that she'd chosen a different world? Entitled or not, he knew he had never loved anyone as he'd loved her. And maybe she'd loved *him* too much, too worshipfully – Ailsa once told him that Skye used to flush with excitement when she heard his car coming – till she was twelve, and the scales were ripped off.

The geese came round again, crying forlornly, clear silhouettes against the livid western horizon that was Toronto.

"And I've watched them under the Northern Lights," he raged.

Only power failures would ever restore true darkness here.

The geese kept circling, unsettled. *"P'iu!"* Twenty yards ahead, Ben had stopped and was aiming one arm at the birds. *"P'iu, P'iu, P'iu!"* his face grimacing as he loosed off phantom shots.

"Ben!" Larry's voice was sharp, but the boy ran on again.

"It's useless," Skye said, "we've tried everything. No war toys, no cop shows – it's just in their blood. *Your* blood!" Larry laughed fondly and pulled her closer.

"There's nothing more innocent than make-believe murder." But Jimmy mumbled it to himself, he didn't want an argument.

Ben came running back to them: "I don't like this part," he said, and went towards his father, but seeing his parents absorbed and arm in arm, he took Jimmy's hand again.

"What's the problem?" Jimmy put his right hand for a moment over the boy's. "It's wild," Ben whispered. "It's tangled up and spooky."

Their short-cut between the two wedges of suburb had kinked to the left, and now they faced a hundred or so yards of unlit dirt road, rutted and potholed, with loose stones and half-frozen puddles. There was a ditch smell in the air, a bitter stagnancy. The lights from the subdivision up ahead made a strange jungle, almost a film-set, of the field to their right where clumps of poplars and wild plum stood out among the overgrown mounds of masonry and surrounded the stone foundations, intact still six feet above the ground, of an old barn.

As they passed the first thicket, something went crashing off through the underbrush. Jimmy could hear the double *thump-thump* of a startled deer. Ben clutched his arm and burrowed against him: "It's a bear, Grandad, it's a bear, isn't it?" You could almost hear the boy's heart knocking in his chest.

"No," Jimmy said, "not at all. It was a deer running off, scared out of its wits, here –" and he bent and hoisted his grandson, turning him with some effort till he was perched on his shoulders. "The wild things don't know yet that this is a town." The boy clutched Jimmy's head, his ankles securely gripped by his grandfather's hands: "Look at me!" he shouted.

Larry came up to them: "You okay like that, Jimmy? He's quite a weight, he's getting too much for *me*."

"I'm fine," Jimmy said, walking on, "I'm not senile yet."

"Father, let Larry take him –"

"I like it with Grandad," Ben cried. "He's taller!"

"It was me put the notion of bears in his head," Jimmy said. "What did that fool say? 'We must bear our cross'!"

Skye's smile, in the orange wash of the approaching lights, was a girl's again. Jimmy and Ben strode on ahead; "Sit still, darling," Skye called.

Something was nagging at Jimmy's mind: words and a voice half-remembered, something about the Bear turning up in our minds. Who the hell was it?

Ben started humming again, then broke into "We three kings." The adults joined in. "Where's Orientar, Grandad?" he asked, as they came out on the first street. "Close to you, and far from me," Jimmy said, but the boy didn't answer. By the time they were half down the block he was asleep, lolling over on Jimmy's head.

Jimmy was thinking of the times he had walked with Skye and Ailsa, along the Saugeen, with Anton upon his shoulders just like this. There used to be an ad in *The Telegraph* each Sunday, some life insurance company, of a young couple, with two children, one on the father's shoulders, and a great cross marked over the father's chest. *"Heart attack can happen at any time"* read the caption. Jimmy had always turned the page quickly, he'd a horror of his children watching him, jerking like a marionette out of control into death in front of them. He'd wanted to paint that picture, but superstition prevented him. In art, there are too many self-fulfilling prophesies.

And now they were back. The house wasn't *so* bad, he supposed: pretty as a Christmas card now with red and green spotlights playing on it from the garden. Yes, *pretty*. All cosmetics. But at least Skye still had a feeling for trees, however tamed these mulberries and other weepers might be.

He carried Ben up to bed, while Larry drove the babysitter home and Skye brought the little girl down to feed. Ben did not awake, and Jimmy just pulled off his pants and sweater, and slipped him under the covers. Even so, he held his breath as he kissed the boy goodnight.

He went into the bathroom. Once in a while it took him five minutes to finish a pee. That's how old age was defined for most of them, he thought. What never got said was how much, too much, you ended up living with. All the worries, and all the guilts about *not* worrying. There just wasn't room for all that if you wanted to go on with a life of your own.

On the mantle in Skye's bedroom was a picture of Ailsa; beside that a snap of Skye, maybe 13 or 14, standing with Anton by the hen house. They'd wanted to call Ben Anton, and Jimmy had faked indifference, so Ailsa had said "No." If he'd protested, she would have said "Yes."

Skye was on the love-seat, bent over the child at her breast, crooning. Jimmy sat next to her, staring at the tiny hands, the glistening lips flecked with white curds, as Skye changed sides and wiped the baby's chin.

"Your breasts are just like your mother's," he said.

"No they're not," she said. "Ailsa's nipples are like doorbells."

"Hmm," he said, "It was meant as a compliment."

The baby sighed, and fastened onto the right breast. "Do you still have a scar?" he asked, "Where my turps fell over and burned you."

Skye smiled and nodded. She tilted her left breast, there was an island of paler skin, about three inches long. He kissed his old fingers, and touched them ruefully to the spot.

"You made that book, for me," she said, "My very own comic book. You came and sat by my bed and drew me three or four new pictures every day."

"I'd forgotten."

"You weren't such a bad dad, you know," she shifted the child in the crook of her arm, "back then."

"Do you still have it?"

She looked down. She was developing little frown lines, vertical, between her eyes. "It's somewhere," she said vaguely. "I must dig it out some day and show it to Ben."

He heard the garage door close, and then Larry came in, throwing his coat on a chair.

"Well," he said, "I'm off to bed, if you don't mind. You have to grab what sleep you can around here. I'll do Ben's stocking when I go up."

He walked to the back of the love-seat, and held out his hand. "Well Happy Christmas, Jimmy – we're glad you could be with us."

Jimmy half rose and took his hand. They stared into each other's baffled eyes. "I suppose I ought to be grateful," he said, "And I am." Skye's eyes were upon him.

Larry bent and kissed the crown of Skye's head, stroking the little girl's cheek as he did so. "Sleep well, princess," he said, "Sleep deep." And to Skye: "See you soon." And went up.

Skye burped the baby at her shoulder. "Why don't you go to bed, Father?" she said. "I'll be a few more minutes."

"Don't feel like it," he said. "If it won't bother you, I'll put another log on the fire and sit up."

"Suit yourself," she got up, kissed him on the cheek, and held the baby for a kiss. "Happy Christmas," she murmured, "see you in the morning. Don't forget to turn the tree-lights off."

Jimmy moved the fire-screen, and reached for one of the cherry-logs he'd brought down for them. But he stood instead and looked round the room.

Everything alien from his world, in Skye's cool good taste. The little painting inside the door – he'd done that when Skye was 17, when he was still using colour – that was the only thing he could feel for. He went to it. It was good and, of course, seemed to be by a stranger. And the red blue and green cast of the Christmas tree lights gave it a strange flatness. She probably thought it belonged to her after all these years, but he'd only lent it.

That and the love seat. The strange side-steps by which things moved. It had been Cat's, and when he'd left her for Ailsa it had stayed with him, and when she'd left him she'd taken it, and now it was Skye's.

He sat back down, and at that moment remembered the phrase he'd been nagged by, walking from church. The bear in the mind, the bear in the woods. It was Gray, Cat's husband, who'd come home from his lectures and sit with his wife and her young art college friends and drink Scotch, and show every sign of enjoying them all. When Jimmy had no idea that her bright glances meant real interest, when he'd no notion that Gray was already a dying man. But then she hadn't known either.

Gray had leaned back in his wing-chair, with Cat on the floor at his knee smiling up across the hearth at Jimmy, Jimmy on this very loveseat where a few months later they would enter into love and confusion. In his ironic, Hart House voice, Gray had observed "You see, the moment we'd hunted the Bear from the woods, He turned up in our minds." There he was.

Jimmy felt under the front of the loveseat, and worked a finger under Skye's smoke-grey upholstery. By God, it was still there, the old blue brocade, like a second skin. Still perhaps with the stains of his lovemaking with Cat, with Ailsa, with others. Did the couch still hug to itself the echoes of the women's cries, or the imprint of Anton's little body?

Oh Christ, he was old. He kneeled at the hearth and put on a log for his old bones. The bark flared and sputtered for a minute, the shadows flew out in the room. He held out his hands to the warmth, stranger's hands. All the guilt and clutter of a lifetime.

He heard footsteps in the bedroom above, then the sound of running water. He went to the cupboard behind the loveseat, and poured himself three fingers of rye. His mind was at work. Whenever he was going to sleep he said prayers of protection, not really prayers, more – visualisations, for everyone who still mattered. He called them up in precisely the same order each time, touching the wood of his bedstead, behind his pillow, as he did so. He even put out protection for Anton.

And he'd suddenly realised that the faces he summoned each night formed a map, a picture. He'd do an etching; yes, by God, he hadn't worked with a plate for five years, he loved the craft of it, the time it used up. And there they'd all be, in order, Anton almost transparent, yes, it would sit like a family tree, but foreshortened. Yes.

He looked past his hand at the fire. Running along the top of the log was a woodlouse, questing here and there, baffled by the heat and the licking flames. His grandmother had called that "Robin Hood's Steed," the first bug on the Yule Log; she told him that Robin Hood came out of the Greenwood astride a great stag at Christmas. You must not rescue it.

He drank. He would make a sketch of that etching. Maybe he should do it now, while it was hatching. But he'd disturb them, rummaging around in his room.

He raised his glass to whatever and drank again. Maybe this etching would lay the ghosts. And he could be free for a while.

He fumbled in his pocket. There, among the various small treasures and amulets, was his true touchstone. The oval wood-gall he'd torn from the old linden tree by the hen-house. The same tree which must have watched Anton dragged and trampled down the pasture. After all this time it was smooth and glossy, the bark still intact. He took it out and held it on his right palm in the firelight.

Whenever he feared, whenever specific dread or vague feelings of doom came over him for himself or the ones who mattered, he would reach in his pocket and touch this knobbly thing. He dreaded its loss more than anything else in the world. But he looked at it now as though it were full of poison, as if it had taken into itself all the loss and agonies which he had used it to avert.

Perhaps it was used up too: too pregnant with grief to have power anymore.

He heard steps on the stairs, and Skye stood at the doorway, her housecoat clutched against her.

"You still up, Father?"

He looked back at the fire, his right hand clenched. "I'm not disturbing you surely? I thought you'd be long asleep."

"Hannah wouldn't settle. She's down now though. But you'll have to be up early, you know. Ben will be screaming around."

He still did not look at her. "Didn't anyone tell you that old people don't sleep well?"

"Suit yourself. But don't be a bear in the morning!" And then, quietly, "Jimmy," she said, and then didn't say.

He heard her climb the stairs and walk overhead. He heard the bed creak and the murmur of voices. He waited for the sounds of their lovemaking, but they did not come.

He passed the touchstone to his left hand, and slipped it back in his pocket. Then he walked round the room, turning off all the lights, till only the tree was left on and he had to get down on his hands and knees to pull its cord from the socket.

In the firelight he went back to the cupboard and poured another drink.

He sat, leaning forward on his knees; the fire twisted and swam through the glass of whiskey. He sipped, and stared some more. His mind was almost empty now, almost clear.

"I won't be here for ever," he told the hearth and, to himself, "I guess the ghosts can look after themselves."

He reached again into his pocket for the touchstone. He looked at it only briefly – it had become a stranger.

He stretched forward and dropped it behind the Yule Log. The heat against his hand was intense.

He leaned back in the love-seat and breathed out. He held the glass to his lips and closed his eyes.

Dusty
Bluebells

THE DOOR OPENED SO QUIETLY behind me that I jumped when he spoke, and I think that decided him that I was shaken up enough, because he just nodded for me to sit down again. Then there was a silence. I tried to meet his eyes without provocation, and he stared back, shaking his head and exhaling sadly.

He was different from the others — in plain clothes for one thing, a light brown suit, and older too, more refined. I didn't know, was I supposed to break the silence? He picked up another chair from beside the door and brought it over, one-handed. He set it down by mine, put a notepad on the bed, and sat facing me.

His eyes were grey, with yellow intrusions. He leaned forward, planting his hands on his knees. The fingers were blunt, but surprisingly delicate. On his wedding finger was a gold, masonic ring.

—"*Facio*." he said.

—"Sorry?"

—"*Facio*."

—"Facio?"

—"That's the one," he said, "the verb, to make or do. How does it go again?"

—"What, *Facio*?" I felt rattled and stupid, and there were signs of

131

impatience in his tightening lips. "You mean, *facio, facere, feci, factum?*"

He stared back coldly for a moment, then his mouth relaxed. — "Yes, *facio*," he said, "you're right on each count. Let's try *sum*, shall we, it's a quare one, is it not?"

—"It is," I said, "it's *sum, esse, fui, sint.*"

—"Ah yes," he sighed, his eyes lazily traversing the bare walls. And he sighed again, and shook his head wearily.

I was still pretty shaken up by my do with the Sergeant. I couldn't stand much of this stuff. —"Why are you asking me all this?"

You'd think he'd have said that it wasn't my place to ask questions, but instead he turned and picked up the yellow notepad. He read from it, though he must have had it by heart, for his eyes wouldn't stay off mine the whole time:

—"'In the outer left hand pocket of his haversack were found a .32 calibre automatic pistol, apparently of Czechoslovakian manufacture, two ammunition clips containing seven bullets each, a Mars bar, and a book, apparently in some foreign language, closely annotated in pencil, and bearing on the title page the words *Agricola* and *Tacitus*.'

...It's the Tacitus that interests me at this moment," he said. "Something of a scholar on the side, are you?"

—"It's for a test," I said, "an exam. We were to read it over the summer, and there'll be a test the first week."

—"You're sticking by that story, are you? On your way to school is it?"

—"It's true," I said, "I promise you."

His eyebrows were sardonic. —"And where would this school be?"

—"Where I told the sergeant. Boltby, in the north of England."

—"That would be near Liverpool, I suppose." —"No, near Newcastle. I told him that too."

He put the notepad back on the bed and flexed his fingers. —"Alright, sonny jim," he said, and seemed to stifle a yawn, "Your home's in Farranfaw, County Kerry in the Republic, and you're on your way to a school in England, hitchhiking through Northern Ireland with an English accent and carrying a deadly weapon. Would you believe that if you were me?"

—"But it's true. I cashed in my train ticket to Dublin to save some money and got a ride with a chap — "

—"That would be Mr McCutcheon?" he interjected, "the *gentle-man* in whose car you were apprehended at the border?"

—"Yes, sir," I said. "He was turning off the Dublin road at Mulingar and going all the way up to Dandalk. I thought I could get the Larne ferry and make it over to England just as fast."

—"When does your school term start?"

—"On Tuesday."

—"Mmm. And what will they think at your school about this business?"

I didn't have an answer for that.

He tapped me on the knee — he wanted my eyes back. "And what will your parents think about this business?"

—"Oh God," I said, "do they have to be told?"

—"Well what do you think?" he said disgustedly. "Are you scared of what your Dad'll have to say?"

—"It's not my father I'm worried about, it's my mother. Her heart." I think he savored the ambiguity of that, but he didn't press me on it. He looked sideways, over at the notepad:

—"Your father's a soldier?"

—"Well he was, yes. He just retired last year."

—"The British Army you say?"

—"Yes. The Green Howards."

—"That's a fine regiment," he said accusingly. "Where was he stationed last?"

—"In Malaya, sir, and before that Burma."

—"Mm. They have their own little troubles in Malaya, I've been reading. Were you out there with him?"

—"Yes. I was in school there for two years."

—"And now they have you to school in England. That would be a catholic academy I imagine?"

—"No, sir, it's not. There's only five of us catholic there...My father doesn't believe in catholic education."

—"Well he has some sense then." He gave off a slightly scented air — it must have been from the soap he used, but it seemed incongruous in this place and in his job. He might have been fifty-five or so — his hair was grey enough in places.

—"Well you have yourself in some scrape here," he said, "whether there's any truth in your story or not."

—"It *is* true," I muttered. But I was just realizing how bad the "scrape" really was. That was 1957 and though the border crossing had looked like a toy fortress, no one would have guessed in those quiet times that the old nightmare of Ulster would reawaken thirteen years down the road. All the same, the myth of the gunman was still potent, and to be caught with a gun —

—"Where'd you get it?" he snapped, as though he could see into my thoughts.

—"The gun, you mean?"

—"The gun, the gun, yes the gun of course, don't be wasting my time and public money. *Where*?"

—"I got it from my brother-in-law."

—"And where's he?"

—"Oh he's out in Canada, and I'd sooner he wasn't involved in this matter."

—"You have no choice, my son, as to who is involved and who isn't. No choice at all."

—"Look," I blurted. "He got it in Berlin after the war for a pound of coffee; and he couldn't take it back to Canada so he left it in a drawer at home and I found it."

—"Are you telling me those bullets are ten years old?"

—"At least that, I'm sure."

—"Have you fired the gun at all?"

—"Just twice, sir. The first round was a dud, and the second just sort of foozled and went halfway up the barrel. I had to push it through with a knitting needle."

He hooked his elbow over the chairback and gave me a sort of smile. His teeth were white and even, well cared for. —"A knitting needle," he said, and nodded a couple of times. "Now no liar would have thought of *that* detail."

But in a way I was lying. For after trying a dozen shells, and only one with any sign of life in it, I'd had the fancy to play a sort of Russian roulette with it. Fired it off at my head in our kitchen. I did it twice and for some reason the third time I aimed it across the room instead. And the damn thing went off and shattered my mother's mirror and left me trembling in that echoing room full of the stink of cordite, and a whole lot of explaining to do when they came home.

—"I don't know," the man said, and he was looking as far into me as you could imagine, with those grainy eyes that must have pierced a thousand pathetic masks through the years. And I wondered what he saw. "I don't know," he repeated. "You'd think an army boy at least would have more sense. Does having a gun along make you feel more of a man?" I shrugged. He made a schoolmasterly gesture with his index finger. –"This is no toy you've been carrying about with your school books. This damned country has seen enough young fellers at that game — you shouldn't credit what you hear in them eejit rebel songs or what you see in Hollywood fillums. Had you ever seen a man struck with a bullet, like I have and your dad too, likely enough, there'd be no glamor in it for ye."

I looked down and acted as crestfallen as I could. Something told me he was starting to trust me. I might even get away with it. But I was thinking about the time our school convoy was ambushed in Malaya, and our trucks raced through and then the armored car went back blazing away. And those two little bandits running out of the jungle almost on top of us, and the bren gun on the carrier opening up. They were only twenty feet away from us, two little Chinese figures dancing on their buttocks down the bankside with bone chips and flaming wads of cotton leaping out around them onto the wet leaves. And two of us throwing up over the back of the truck. But cycling down from school the next weekend to hunt for souvenirs.

–"What about this Agricola?" He asked, and turned to pick up the notepad again. "It seemed to me desperate hard stuff to wade through."

–"Well it's Silver Latin," I said, trying hard not to sound smartassed. "Not as simple as Caesar and those writers. Agricola was the general who put down the rebellions in Britain."

–"I'd hazard a guess," he said, and he gave a little smile, "that he never made it as far as Ireland."

–"No, he was mostly fighting the Welsh — the druids and all."

–"It's a rum thing, that their writers were all soldiers, isn't it?"

–"I never thought of that," I said, restraining my growing cockiness. He believed me, I was sure. I thought I was off the hook. "Are you a Latin scholar yourself, sir?"

–"Me? No." He ruffled the notepad abruptly and stood up. "I'm an ignorant man. Only what little I've taught myself." And he looked candidly down at me. This was the moment — I could sense it. "But I know the value of an education, and I'm thinking what a terrible waste it is for a lad with your opportunities to end up a criminal when your dad's given you such a chance."

The silence was terrific. I tried to put my face into a shape that would match whatever he was thinking.

He moved to the door. His shoes had crepe soles. "You'll have a

long night to think all this over," he said, "and so will I. There'll be
a meal of sorts along bye and bye. Do you need anything here?"

–"Could I have my cigarettes back?"

He shook his head again: –"You'd think with the stuff that's
coming out now about those things, a bright youngster like you
would know better. Ah well."

And then, just before the door shut, he looked in again. –"Civis
Romanus sum?" It came out like a question. –"Sunt lacrimae
rerum," I shot back and then cursed my cheek. But he just pursed
his lips and murmured, –"I wouldn't doubt it," and closed the door.

The constable who brought in my cigarettes couldn't have been
more than twenty. He had big hands and feet and jug-ears and I
think it was the first time a policeman had ever looked young to me.
The plainclothesman must have said something to him because he
was altogether more relaxed than they'd been when I was brought
in. Inclined to be friendly, in fact. –"Your supper will be down sune,"
he said, "but here's a mug of tea will keep you going." He turned
the cigarette pack over in his hand: "Sweet Aftons eh, I never had
one of them southern cigarettes." I had one lit in a flash –"Help
yourself if you like," I said. "Try one."

–"I wouldn't mind at that," he said. And after a long pull he told
me they were dry to his taste but no worse than a Woodbine. "How
much now would these cost in the Republic?" he asked. –"Oh, two
and six," I said. He whistled: –"It may be a poor country but it's a
cheap one, then. Two and six! — why twenty Players'd put you
back four and twopence here."

–"Yes, I suppose the six counties are the same as England when
it comes to prices." A cigarette had never tasted this good to me —
and I hoped he wouldn't leave. I liked him.

–"The six counties?" he said. "Now don't you be talking like a
republican, Paddy, or you'll make things worse for yourself.
Northern Ireland is the only name for it here."

–"I meant no harm," I said. "It's just what I'm used to." He was in
a hurry to forgive me. –"Don't you let your tea get cold now — I put
four spoons of sugar in it for you." And then, "Must be a scare for
you to wind up in this place."

He was right there. It wasn't at all what I'd have expected. My
cousin Eugey Fleming got six months in Tralee for dynamiting the
salmon, and he was down to Dineen's Bar every night of the week
keeping Sgt. Keogh company. Eugey could hold his liquor better
than the sergeant so he'd help him home each night, get him into

the house so Mrs Keogh wouldn't hear, and then lock himself into the cell for the night. It was all a joke really. But this was a different world altogether — it smelt like a barracks, and the cops were mostly ex-soldiers, and I didn't like to think what their real prisons might be like.

The constable told me I could call him Bob when there was no one around. He seemed in no hurry to leave and I was grateful for his company after the last few hours. I offered him another Afton.

–"You're very generous," he said and then his blue farmboy eyes looked uneasily at me: "You wouldn't be trying to get round me now, would you?"

–"Of course not." I put on my most guileless face. "I'm just glad of the company. I've never been in a place like this before."

He sat down then; he couldn't resist being kind. And with a sort of grotesque try at a knowing wink, he whispered –"Between ourselves, Paddy, I think they will let you go tomorrow. The Super said for us to go easy on you, that he believed your tale." After which he affected a stern and puritan look and said, "I hope now his trust won't be misplaced?"

It was then that there was a loud crash down the corridor — the clash of a metal door followed by a kind of strangled cry. Constable Bob hastily butted out his smoke and went to the cell door, straightening his tunic. And behind him for a moment I saw two policemen and a pale man in a dark coat. He was stooped over and they were dragging and kicking him along, roaring out curses. My constable followed them and I heard the door of the next cell flung back, a great smacking noise and a voice in a high register crying out –"Please don't hit me. Please. There's no need for that." The grating voice of the sergeant then, the red-faced bastard who had scared me half to death that afternoon. –"No need, is it? Why I just might *kill* you, you perverted little weasel," and a yelp of pain and something thudding against the wall.

My friend was back in the doorway, shaking his head, his mouth set virtuously. –"What's happening?" I asked. –"Oh it's a bad business, Paddy — the worst kind. It's a child mo-lester they've brought in." A high wavering squeal came down the corridor and then a great burst of laughter, and in at our door came another constable, almost reeling with mirth, crying –"Oh jesus jesus, Bobby, wait till you've seen this!"

He was holding a gigantic penis. It must have been eighteen inches long and four inches thick. And he passed it to my friend:

"Would you credit that, man!" his face crimson with stifled laughter. He looked over at me and crooked his finger: "Come and take a look; you'll be green with envy, my son, for the rest of your days."

It looked especially grotesque in the hand of my innocent friend. It was made from a strip off a side bacon, rolled up and tied with string so that the yellow skin showed, and lashed to the end of it was a sheep's heart. –"The crazy bugger had it stowed in his trousers — he was flashing it at the kiddies up the Dovetow Rec."

He grinned at me and winked: –"Exhibit A, for you my son. We'll leave it in your keeping for a while — might be the IRA's secret weapon." Then his smile took on a different cast: "Come on along, Bob, and help us do him over."

–"No I'll stay," my friend said, looking down. "You go along Fergus, I'm alright here." The other gave him a contemptous glare and left. The ruckus built up again in the next cell — shouting and protests — and we were left there, Constable Bob and me at the cell door, and he with that cold meat artifact in his hands.

–"They're giving him a rough time in there," I said. –"Ay, well it's nothing to what they'll do to him in prison." –"But you're not going to touch him, are you?" –"Ah no," he sighed and his eyes searched mine to see if I, too, would accuse him of weakness: "Why would I want to hurt the man — he can't be right in the head. I'd feel differently I suppose, if I'd children of my own." And then he looked down at the thing in his hands, and back at me with a kind of sheepish, incredulous grin.

Then the Super was striding past, his brown suit jacket undone and flapping. He didn't cast a glance at us, and I heard him bark out –"Alright now, leave him be. It's my turn."

The Sergeant and Fergus came grinning back, both breathing heavily, and the Sergeant grabbed the penis and swung playfully at my head with it. "You'll have some tale to tell the scholars alright," he said, and beamed as if I were now one of the boys. And this was the man who three hours earlier had held me up against the wall by my shirt collar and breathed his foul breath over me, and spat in my face and cursed: –"You're one of Rossiter's pretty boys, ain't you? Who're you with, McCann is it? Dillon?" And repeatedly and viciously he had slapped me, forehand and back across the face, calling me a murderous little cunt. I had wet myself with fear and shame.

The three of them went off with their prize.

I walked around the cell, restless. From time to time I heard from next door that sound they never get right in the movies — one man's flesh colliding baldly with another's. But now there was only a sustained crooning note in response, a soft sad lullaby-like crooning. And that dead flesh sound cutting in upon it for another minute or two before a chair clattered against the floor and the cell door slammed.

For the second time I didn't notice him till he was already in the room with me. He was watching me, and fastidiously adjusting his shirt cuff. He breathed lightly, but there was a fretting of sweat on his brow and a sheen on his upper lip.

–"Well me bould Fenian boy," he said (and I knew then that Constable Bob had been right, that I'd soon get off scot free). "I just had a visit from Mr McCutcheon."

–"The man who gave me the ride?"

–"The *gentle*man," he said. "Charles McCutcheon is a company director, and you're the one has put him in a very delicate position, wouldn't you say?"

–"Is he in trouble over this?" I asked.

–"Charles McCutcheon? — oh certainly not. He's well known in these parts, and a very influential man. But *you* may be surprised to know that he went out of his way to come down and put in a good word for you. He told me he thought you were alright, and that you'd impressed him, he said."

It didn't surprise me at all actually. He'd likely been in a sweat all day: I might have blurted out that after buying me lunch and three beers in Drogheda, he'd driven in by the gatehouse of a ruined estate and offered me five pounds if I'd be "naughty" with him. The fiver was hidden in my left sock and it didn't look like they'd be searching me any more thoroughly now than they had already.

–"I'll be thinking it over," the Super said. "You have a good night now. Think about something wholesome, if you've any sense." –"I wouldn't mind something to read," I told him. –"I'll send something down," he said. "And don't be paying no mind to this pother next door. The world's an uglier place, my son, than you need to know about." And he was gone.

I went to sleep that night with the smug feeling that all this drama would simply become a great story to tell at school, with me as the hero. And probably no one would believe it. But something woke me in the dark hours and I lay there, cold and fearful for more

than an hour, convinced they'd been fooling me, and that more
shame and pain would break over me in the morning. I felt terribly
small and alone, and I remember wondering if the man in the next
cell was lying awake too, and what he was thinking. And for a little
while I wished I could talk to him.

A policewoman brought me breakfast, and when she came back
for the tray she said the Super wished to see me in his office, and
she pointed to the right down the corridor.

The man next door was sitting on the edge of his bed. I could see
that his left eye was puffed up and his nose swollen, and one sleeve
of his jacket was ripped free of its lining. His hands lay clasped in
his lap and he looked shyly towards me, sideways, where I stared in
through the Judas window. I couldn't fathom that look at the time:
it was almost buffoonish. It was both appealing and defiant,
hunted and past shame, self-mocking and gentle. The face, I now
realise, of a political prisoner, a prisoner of conscience. An outlaw
brought in from the wilderness with nothing but his own vanishing,
discredited dreams to sustain him.

My pistol lay on the Super's desk, beside the ammo clips and the
tattered red Tacitus, which was open. –"Sit down," he said, and
pushed the book across to me. He spoke ruefully: "I'll never get the
hang of it, I began too late. I'll never get to read the books — it
frustrates me something fierce, that."

Then, as I took my book and closed it: "Your haversack is in the
charge room." And he left just enough silence to start me
squirming again. "I have a driver going up to Belfast in ten
minutes — he'll take you to the bus station. You'll make the noon
crossing from Larne I daresay."

I said –"Thank you," and fixed him with all the innocent
gratitude I could coax into my big blue eyes. I had the knack of
making myself look more like twelve than sixteen.

–"Right," he said. "On your way then." He stood and took off his
jacket and, as he folded it neatly over his chair's arm, he fished out
a new ten shilling note from the breast pocket and held it out.
"Here, buy yourself some lunch on the steamer." He was close to
being embarrassed.

–"You've been awfully good to me," I said. For a moment I
thought he might be rethinking it all, but it was just the habit of
his eyes: –"We could have made trouble for you," he said, "and
then it would have been trouble for the rest of your days." He

walked round the desk, "I'll come a bit of the way with you," he said.

I could smell that perfumed soap or whatever as he came close. He started unbuttoning his cuffs as we went out the door together, and rolled up one sleeve over a surprisingly thick, sandy forearm. "After a while," he said, "you learn to trust your judgement in this game." And he rolled up his other sleeve. "So don't let me down." And before I could reply, he stopped at the locked cell and squinted in at the Judas window. It was as though he'd forgotten me already. He put a key in the lock and turned it. I stepped softly off down the corridor.

The corporal who drove me up was a cherry, wisecracking man in his thirties, recently demobbed from the Ulster Rifles and full of yarns about Cyprus and Aden and his wife and two youngsters. I didn't have to talk much and it was only about ten-thirty when we came in at the outskirts of Belfast. A desolate, grey, poverty-stricken, crowded, hazy, stone-faced city I thought it, and our route took us through the worst parts of it. Narrow streets, shabby people and stores and a strange blend of coalsmoke and sea in the air. It felt as though it had rained there every day of the year.

We pulled up at the end of a red-bricked terrace street, outside a small police station on the corner. –"I shouldn't be too long," the corporal said, "do you want to come inside?" –"No," I said, "I'll wait." He got out and took the three steps to the station door at one bound. He left the keys in the ignition.

A gang of children were playing across the intersection in a vacant lot where an end house had been pulled down. You could still see the wallpapers exposed to the weather, the zigzag white scar where the stairs had been and, in one room on the top floor, the faded place where a bed had stood against the wall, and a dressing table with a mirror.

There must have been twenty or twenty-five children in all, split into two loose groups, running and playing. I rolled down the car window and lit a cigarette and heard the girls' voices as they clapped and chanted:

> *Green gravel, green gravel*
> *Your grass is so green*
> *You're the fairest young damsel*
> *That ever I've seen...*

There was a bit of a sea breeze cruising between the houses, and it lifted the edge of a half-sheet of newspaper and rolled it over the curb and off around the legs of the skipping youngsters.

> *I washed her, I kissed her*
> *I dressed her in silk*
> *And I wrote down her name with*
> *A black pen and milk...*

A little girl came out of a house across from the car, and stood in the doorway, in her meagre print dress, swinging on one foot and watching me. I glinted my eyes in a mock-fierce face and blew smoke out of my nose like a dragon. Her hands went up to her face and then crawled into a finger-lattice over her eyes. I looked away from her and back again, away and back, until with a high giggle she ran straight over to the derelict lot, her flimsy dress blowing against her thin legs, her arms outstretched and trailing behind her, like the wings of a small bird. She joined a knot of her friends and they all looked back at the police car for a moment. Two of them answered my wave and then they were off together across the waste lot, moving with all the joyous gravity of their tribe towards the other children.

There was a rap at the driver's window. A constable was there, his tunic unbuttoned and without a hat. —"Corporal says for you to come inside and have a cup of tea. He'll be a while yet, he says."

—"Will I lock the car?" I asked.

—"Ach no," he said, puzzled. "Why would you do that?"

He turned back to the station steps and I got out on my side and slammed the door.

Some little squabble on the empty lot had been resolved and all the children were forming into one band, moving and singing in a snaking line that weaved in and out of itself

> *In and out the dusty bluebells*
> *In and out the dusty bluebells*
>   girls and boys together.

There were no slogans on the walls back then, no young English soldier at each street corner with his Armalite held at the ready, no armored cars dashing through the intersections every twenty minutes. Just that little wasteland of brick-shards and dead earth, with the odd clump of nettles and a few weeds, willow-herb or wallflower, pointing up from the rubble.

But for all that, the children were playing on the emerald

Greensward, out in the open between the houses and the endless grim line of the Wildwood.

> *In and out the dusty bluebells*
> *In and out the dusty bluebells*
> *In and out the dusty bluebells*
> *Won't you be my darling?*

Their game drew them further from their houses, always closer to the forest's dark wall. And out of the trees stepped the ogre, towering and wide-legged, and stood there pale and watching, swinging his monstrous club.

We ran and we played and our voices flew up, clear and unformed, across the meadow, through the bright air:

> *Green gravel, green gravel*
> *Your grass is so green*
> *You're the fairest young damsel*
> *That ever I've seen.*

And that figure from the Wilderness stood there, alone and waiting, and played out his oafish role: wagging his clumsy abomination to and fro in the face of our innocence.

Snake Oil

THE BOMBS WERE COMING from the north-east, out of the swamp, falling from the wings and bellies of the silver jets. Three planes, at tree level, and from each a dark cluster of bombs, a glimpse of them dropping like turds through the strip of sky above the jungle. One landed intact thirty yards away and skipped, upending, towards the shade trees. The rest were flame behind and a shuddering in the earth while the jets screamed up towards the hills. A burro plunged into the square, with a hindquarter adrift, its empty panniers flapping. The sound of the jets ebbed off to the south, and then throbbed back upon the air. The square was filled with their afterwave, a monstrous crying of doves. Then silence seeped into the valley. The men's clubhouse collapsed.

A few feet to his left a crowd of ants was busy upon a pig's foot, turned up from the dust by his cart wheel. They swarmed through the stiff cleft of the trotters, braiding themselves like a rope of wild currants. From all directions a tide of ants lipped through the dust towards them. He lay with his cheek to the earth, arms braced, waiting for the jets to come back. His cart was undamaged; the mules were still standing, tethered beside the shafts to a red wall. There was no movement in the village, only the ants by his face and the mule tails flicking the air. Ten minutes passed. The combined assault of the ants had shifted the pig's foot – it toppled onto its back, a delicate, crusted hoof. The planes were not returning.

There was a rush into daylight of feet and voices – families with children and sacks of possessions were running clumsily behind the houses, onto the back road towards the cane fields. Part of the herd passed his cart – he watched unseen the bare feet and wide cotton trousers scissoring and stumbling away from the danger which had passed. A grey dog with a torn ear stopped at the sight of the ants and trotted towards the cart. It checked when it saw him there, lifted its leg to mark the wheel rim, and nosed forward.

Once he had worked miracles. Now he hugged the dead earth beneath a cart while the peasant herd stampeded towards the hills, the ants swarmed upon carrion, a dog pissed against his wheel. Why would anyone waste bombs on such a place – seventy hovels, four hundred mindless peasants, *iguanas* – and why when he was doing busines here? He had barely unyoked the mules when the first bombs sounded in Matorno across the swamp, and the lizard-eyed fools had run back to their houses. Yes, his life was designed for miracles but they never worked for himself. Else he would not be here in the first place. Or would vanish in this second from so naked a spot, into the hills with his cart and mules. To hell with this life. The dog picked up the pig's foot, ants studding its chops, and tossed its head to get a better grip. It rubbed the ants from its muzzle in two long sweeps against the dirt, insolently before his face. He worked a miracle.

The dog remembered the leaf-mould under the wild bananas, off by the swamp on the rim of its nightly circuit. The dry surface of the leaves and the delicious musk of the fibrous rot beneath, calling out to be rolled upon in a bliss of abandoned puppyhood, sky-belly, shoulder-squirm, yapping to the bull-frog descant of the alligators. Thick, sensual musk. It dropped the pig's foot and trotted off directly, towards the forest. The ants rolled back to the feast.

He crawled out. The square was empty. A few dogs had repossessed the shade, though one was sniffing among the clouds of flies where the burro's blood trail stained the earth. Four or five buzzards were circling low down the swamp road; the shaft of the unexploded bomb stuck out by a root in the swept sand under the acacias.

He made to brush the earth from his thighs, but he had sweated mightily during the attack and the grains of spent soil caked his pants in red streaks. From the wheel of his cart the stream of dog's piss was trailing out into the sun, steaming a little, a sluggish river in miniature, parting the sands as he had seen on the Regagua Delta from his one plane ride. It kept moving across the thirsty dust, as if the dog's bladder had been limitless. Ah no, a fluid was dripping from the cart's axle – a gesture of camphor passed his face: it was the elixir.

Something had crashed through the canopy without his realising. Just above his faded emblem, where the dragon's crimson jaws awaited St. George's mercy stroke, was a rent in the canvas. He climbed up – a piece of shrapnel like a grain scoop sat blue and pitted on his scorched blanket, and the two-gallon drum of elixir lay on its side, oozing at a burst seam. If he had hidden in the cart he would be dead now. He righted the little drum – half the snake oil was gone.

It was a sign alright. Time to give up this life. He would complete this circuit, cut it short even, track straight up the valley to Arbeya and sell the mules. Stay in the city, this country was more fucked up than it had ever been, take a market stall, put his savings into that cantina, find a convent girl to keep house for him.

The mules backed away nervously from the wall – muscle spasms jolting their forequarters. He stared resignation into their brute eyes and led them back to the shafts. He sorted out the shambles inside as best he could. Half of the calico bolts were slick with snake oil – ruined. The shrapnel was still hot when he tossed it overboard. A box of brass bells and angels was spilt across his bed but these he cleared off carelessly with his foot and took up the reins still standing. –"*Vamos.*" The mules lurched forward into the square, their ears laid flat upon their necks.

A ghost town, one kitchen burning, the rest of the white and red adobe walls staring like a mirage into the sunlight. Most of the dogs were sleeping now; the cart bed creaked upon its axles across the little square. Out from the lumber pile of the clubhouse, under the fig tree that shaded the well, a small figure sat, one foot tapping to a slow, irregular rhythm. He called across –"Eh, old man, you too proud to run with the other *iguanas*?" He laughed; a coil of phlegm came up in his throat and he spat it out between the mules' rumps. The figure by the well did not acknowledge, the old foot worked to its own music. "*Sssss* – rouse yourself, grandad! You know me, eh? – Sandro the worker of miracles. Must have heard of me – look, for two *reals* I can give you back your memories. For five I will restore the power of generation..." He pulled the mules over and looked down.

The man was very old. Perhaps a founder of the village in the days of his strength and judgement. Both gone now. His jaw was trembling rapidly, in a palsey at odds with the slow persuasion of the projecting foot. Terror or age had fixed the eyes on a point towards the swamp where the buzzards fell. –"Wake up, old man, they've left you behind.\You want to ride with me to the hills? What you going to do, then, huh – wait for them to run home?" Why should he trouble – one *iguana* was like any other... But there was a sign here, the old man was a sign he did not understand. It was bad, he must alter it.

But to work a miracle he must have their eyes. He reached for his whip and snapped it over the man's hat. The mules flinched, the jaw and the foot by the well did not acknowledge. The whip's third stroke caught the old turkey neck, flicked up the shuddering jaw. Sandro had the eyes – half-cataracted staring out of a milk-cloud. He worked the miracle. The old man slowly drew in his foot and closed his mouth, smiling in beatitude up at the fly-shimmer under the fig leaves. He was reliving the day of his retirement from the fields, into the honored leisure of the clubhouse. He eased his back against the low wall of the well and smiled up still at the insects. The mules turned away towards the gardens.

The best plan would be to take the old silver miners' trail over to the next valley. A long, rough way, but he would avoid the villages: bad for business, good for the health. Who knew where the bombs would fall next – such waste and foolishness. Peasants, sheep, iguanas – these creatures knew nothing of rebellion, or of right and left – war was just war to them: an alien, hungry tide since before the Conquest. They did not count as people – bombs were for people.

There was shooting beyond the canefields. Army guns. So they were following after the bombs, looking for red iguanas – well, they wouldn't trouble him. He turned the mules back into the square, under the shade trees at the west end, and waited. The sun was not impatient, the hours would pass. He pulled the old copy of *La Bandera* from under his blanket; he had read it ten times already this circuit. The price of flour was to be fixed, an oil-find was rumored in the Gulf, the manager of the Spartans was accused of fraud, the rebels in Oriente were blowing up bridges with Cuban dynamite. He turned to the comic pages – *El Fantomas* had been blocked out by the censor, but the American funnies were there, with their slabs of color, orange and yellow and blue. These were very good, the animals especially. The dog with the potato face in *Carlotas*, who chased the baseballs, and the fat cat with eyes of a frog who was the glutton's glutton: this time he was stealing from the man's kitchen and patting his belly. Yes, when he had the cantina in Arbeya he would have the funny pages from America two times a week and share them with his customers. And he would leave the miracles behind him.

The villagers were running back towards the square: a jolting white-clad mob with a jeep at their backs and the foot soldiers herding them. Many had lost their hats, the children were sprinting ahead, they were making no noise. *Iguanas*. He sat with the newspaper spread on his knees, watching the foolishness. The foot soldiers had the small machine guns, and on the jeep was the big Browning, like a grasshopper, that could shoot, they said, a thousand times in a minute.

Perhaps twenty-five soldiers – it was the troop he had passed last week below Constaras, and the captain with the different eyes, and the two young brothers from Guatalpa. All young, except the captain and his driver, fresh from the barracks and showing off with their fancy weapons. How a boy felt changed with a machine gun across his chest. Now, after a week in the hills, they were dusty and stained and wishing they were back in the barracks. Some were barefoot, the natural way for them, out of the stiff prisons of their army boots. *Iguanas*, too, most of them.

The square was filling up with the dull odor of fear – they were herding the men and the children over by the houses, and the women in his direction. That was original, anyway – that captain meants to put the fear of god into them. Two of the soldiers waved towards the cart, recognizing the dragon-killer sign, and walked over. It was the brothers. Back on the road last week they had stood together, holding hands and staring when he brought out the elixir, but now they walked importantly and condescended, aware of their audience.

– "So, is our charlatan making good profits this trip?" The elder brother leant on the cart, in a pose learned from his captain, his eyes wandering to the funny paper. The other lit a cigarette and laughed –"Gaar-feeeild" he said, "Never stops feeding!" Sandro passed the paper down, accepted a cigarette. –"So now you hunt *iguanas* with machine guns?" The elder brother looked up from the comics: –"Rebel *iguanas*," his captain's voice again. "We shot six of them, hiding in the fields." –"Rebels" his brother echoed, smoke eddying from his indian nostrils, "running from the government forces." –"You would not run if the bombs fell on you?" –"Only rebels need fear government forces" it came like a church response. The other giggled –"Eh, Marco, see the cat here, with the noodle hanging from his teeth!"

A shout called their attention back to the square. The elder brother straightened up and shoved the paper back on the seat. He spoke sternly –"You know these people?" Sandro shrugged: –"My first time down this valley. Just *iguanas* like all the others – and your bombs they spoiled my business. They're harmless fools, you waste your time." –"Rebels" said the soldier, "you wait and see. Mother-molesting communistas."

The Captain was standing up in the jeep. They were harboring rebels, he told them, that was common knowledge. Some of them were perhaps rebels, or had sons in the hills. Well, they must point out the rebels to him, the Captain, and then the government soldiers who were here to protect them, would leave them in peace and forget about them harboring the reds. He understood, you see, that they had been frightened into this wickedness, this collaboration, but now they could see that the government had control of the whole province, there was nothing left to fear.

He was very slim and controlled, gesturing occasionally with his thin hands to include the two groups of villagers. He spoke like the schoolteacher, the ex-jesuit, in Sandro's old village, who would never raise his voice for attention but would rather speak quieter and quieter, til every ear in the school-room was straining for his words in silence and dread.

The *iguanas* stared back at the jeep. The Captain reminded them that he and his tireless men had the whole valley to protect and could not have their time wasted. They should point out the rebels, or their sympathisers, immediately. He sat down in the passenger seat. –"You have three minutes," he said. He bit the end from a thin cigar and his driver lit it for him.

Last week, too, the Captain had used up time with a cigar. His right eye was brown and the left was green. Sandro had told him –"You have the luck of the two eyes" and the Captain had stared back and said –"The bullets have never touched my vital places." It would be hard to work a miracle within that one. Soldiers always laughed at Sandro, but they left him alone, and to this troop he had sold two flasks of elixir as well as tobacco and candy. One to the boy with the worm in his tooth, the other to the big recruit from the island whom they'd pushed forward, half proud and half ashamed because he had picked up the pox on his first night's leave in Arbeya. One of them dreamed that night of his first taste of sherbet, when he was four, and the other washed off his corroded skin in the cool shallows of infancy. They had wanted the medicine for nothing, but he'd told them it would not operate without payment and they had laughed and paid. Not knowing that it was his eyes upon theirs, as they took the worthless stone bottles, that worked the cure.

He had told them the story about the peasant and the looking glass, aware that it was their fathers and brothers they were laughing at, and they had picked up his word "*iguanas*" for the villagers and tossed it about. And the Captain, near the end of his cigar, had told him contemptuously —"But you're an *iguana* too" and —"Not so" retorted Sandro, who had learned that the truth is best concealed by itself, "When I was nine years old I learned how to perform miracles and my mind became that of a man." —"Charlatan" the Captain, with his castilian skin, had sneered, and thrown out his cigar butt; and they had gone on, laughing up the trail, calling back *Charlatan*, and jostling each other like footballers.

But God knew the truth of it. When in his tenth year the unclouded voice of alterations had come to him while he was shitting beside the arroyo, and he had turned his father's mind that afternoon away from selling the store and going with the miners. But he had not discovered what to do with the miracles — they had not brought prosperity, even.

The Captain threw out his half-smoked cigar and stepped down from the jeep. He gestured to a villager to grind out the stub with his foot. For a moment every gun was pointing at the man. He trod on the cigar. The Captain looked at his wristwatch and unbuckled his holster —"Now we talk" he said. His voice scarcely carried to the cart. He pointed the revolver at the peasant's foot and then at his head. "If you do not point out a rebel, then I will know you are a rebel yourself." The man stared numbly at the pistol. The Captain fired. A woman and a child screamed together from each group. The two herds recoiled, someone jostled a foot soldier as they backed off. The machine guns were going off all at once, the

silences resolved – the Captain and his driver had to throw them-
selves down. The foot soldiers were grinning like boys on a
fairground, cresting the big wheel.

Sandro had leapt from the cart and was staring under the shafts
into the new, ringing silence. The soldiers were herding the two
groups apart again, kicking up the figures who had been kneeling
over the bodies, dragging the unwounded to their feet. Livid with
rage, the Captain was standing with his pistol arm outstretched
and shaking; beckoning. They brought a man forward, plucking off
the child that clung to his leg.

The man was in his thirties, hatless, a machete hanging loose in
his thick hand. The blade was honed down almost to a bird-wing:
near the tip and the hilt the sun caught the golden patina of corn;
the centre was stained black by sugar cane. The man's eyes were on
the double row of medals over the Captain's heart. The Captain put
the muzzle of his revolver under the man's chin and raised it till
their eyes met.

Name? Galerio. *Age?* Shrug. *Age!* I think thirty-five. *I think
thirty-five! You are a rebel.* Oh no, sir. *It is not a question. I am
telling you, you are a rebel. It is – unwise to contradict. You are quite
foolish.... Family?* Yes. *Family?* Three children, sir. *Where is your
woman?* My wife? *Show me your woman, which one is she? ... Show
me your woman! ... You, there, point to me this minute the wife of
this rebel.*

She was younger, round faced, pure Indian stock. Looking across
for her children. Heavy already with another. Sandro stared at her
across his mules' rumps. *Iguanas* – they breed, they have no minds,
their eyes are shuttered, and against twenty little soldiers they
stand in a great herd, and stare. And that husband there, with his
wicked machete almost a part of his body for thirty years, trying to
avoid the Captain's eyes. Indians. Peasants. *Iguanas.*

Rebels and breeders of rebels. The Captain waved his pistol –
they pulled the woman away, over to the acacia tree in front of the
jeep. They pushed her down against the roots that snaked through
the dust. The sun came in under the leaves upon her. The brothers
looked up; another baton flick from the pistol; they tore open the
cotton dress. The husband stared at the Captain's belt. The
Captain held out his left hand. The husband handed over the
machete.

The driver of the jeep took the long knife, felt its edge and
grinned. He took a black twist of tobacco from his breast pocket and

shaved it upon the jeep's hood with delicate, short strokes of the blade. He tucked the machete under his arm and rolled a cigarette in a strip of corn husk. He lit it. In the husband's face a muscle flickered twice, like the tremors in a mule's hide.

The driver threw the machete towards the shade. One of the brothers reached out to grab it and missed. Its handle bounced off a root and fell by the woman's foot. It was the younger boy – he retrieved the knife and his shadow fell across the naked woman. He looked towards the Captain and held the blade near the woman's chin. Marco, his brother, watched him, and the Captain, and the husband. The blood tide was starting to ebb.

The Captain consulted his watch again. He replaced the revolver in its holster and straightened up –"So," he said, briskly, matter of fact, "now you shall tell me *who* gives your orders, *where* the weapons are hidden, *where* you keep the radio." An insect sound of mindless grief was filling the silence; the Captain turned abruptly away.

His movement conjured energy by the jeep, like a shuttling black wing, and out of it two soldiers stepped, caressing the husband's jaw with the mouths of their carbines. The driver strode across to the trees and took the machete from the staring boy. He knelt beside the woman, with one hand on the back of the blade. The husband's eyes were closed, the eyes of the peons strayed round the square, the old man by the well smiled up at the fruitflies among the fig leaves. Sandro rested his chin on the mule's rump.

Where there should have been intestines was a lump of blue and gold, shifting under the driver's left hand as he searched for a purchase. He dug out a limb from the slick, muscular parcel, and hauled it free, lugging and trimming. The woman's eyes were open. The brothers held her arms but her misery fumbled like hands in the riot of her belly; her eyes, with maternal greed, sought out the sex of her child, watching the boy-thing as it flew from under the tree and landed in the sunlight half way to Sandro's cart, thudding and rolling once on the worn out soil. The double wound of muscle and skin was a huge false vulva, collapsing lopsidedly into her bones. A dog whined and stood up, stretching in its patch of shade.

The driver was standing, his shadow purple among the roots, and the Captain leaned back against the jeep and nodded. The husband had not opened his eyes. The crowd edged back again, and the two soldiers from the husband's side. The driver swung the machete lightly and then darted across, whirling it, with one foot forward. It was the posture exactly of a pitcher in baseball. The husband's knees touched the earth first, and the body fell flat, bleeding like a reptile's. The driver picked up the head by its cropped hair and took it back to the tree. The eyes were open now. He handed it to the younger brother and walked away.

The stillness was like an echo of silence. Then that insect wail again, sighing back through the square from the house fronts or the hills. The boy shoved the head into the woman's open belly. The brothers and all the soldiers stepped back towards the jeep, as if for a curtain call.

The mules' eyes rolled as Sandro stepped past them. There was a voice in his head that he acknowledged with the greatest clarity. Twenty machine guns swung towards him, their muzzles blank eyes upon his face. He walked in the patient sunlight, towards the Captain's eyes, rehearsing the images of his miracle.

Lilith

FOR HOGG

I WOKE TO THE CRY OF THE STONES. The moisture that seeps through my walls was calling me. I can smell it at last, coming: a rumor from the hills, red pollen on the wind. I laugh. The moon was swollen, hump-backed last night; I sprawl through the day – nothing through the high bars but the tense sky, almost white. Never a cloud. The Bride of Christ knows too; she is in ferment all afternoon, screaming *Yes, yes again.* Her moans are a great dough, yeasting out through our forgotten corridor; the air is thick with her endless lust. Evening brings Lubo, with bread and sour wine; he reels at my cell door, sodden, owlish. – "Come out, witch," he growls. He follows me, like a toad's shadow, down the covered lane to empty my bucket. The shrubs round the courtyard know, the cicadas chine vengeance. The Bride is still moaning softly as we pass her door. I call – "Patience, Bride, we'll show them tomorrow." She gasps and curses me and goes back to her rutting. Lubo's thick fingers push down into my rump and force me onwards. Above the midden pit he fumbles up my shift, spreads his flab hands on my thighs and pulls me back against him. His stub of a thing is hard against my ribs, despite his drunkenness. – "Your last day, toad," I murmur. "Tomorrow you go to the wall." – "Move, witch," he sneers, pushing me away and back down the corridor, "It's time for my ration." – "You're getting senile, crab," I shout, running away from him, "I could

155

brain you with this filth-pail" and I throw out "Tomorrow, Bride" as I pass. She shrieks in anger, or is it in holy convulsion? I shriek back, slamming my cell door; he yanks it open and sends me sprawling. His smelly sheep's prick is out in his hand. "I'll yell for Gala," I say. "She'll kill you." He says nothing and comes down, straight into me from long practice. – "There," he grunts, "There, you live for it, you slut." It's hard work for him – he stares and blurts at the damp stones above my head, pumping away. – "Old, Old," I taunt, in ecstasy. He slaps me hard and nearly loses balance – "Don't give me *age*, you devil. I know you" and his rage gets him there, his watery sperm floods out of me. He lies upon me like a squashed rat. – "Never again," I say softly. "They'll haul you off in the morning." I'm watching his old wife Gala in the doorway, mighty in rage. I let fly my last burst for ever of crazy laughter.

Shooting in the streets and squares. Trees whipped by bullets, masonry letting go. Screams in the prison house coming down, stage by stage towards us. The liberation. Doors and the echoing iron and boots. A volley of firing. Now. I see uniforms and young beards, and Lubo, his eyes closed with blood, cringing beside the soldiers. – "Don't trust her," he moans, "She's the devil." Someone has struck him very hard. The young men don't know what to do now. Some are afraid of madness – I see one reach to make the sign of the cross and then stop himself. Others are almost sick with pity and disgust. Two are alight with a pure fire of belief – their faith will blow down this prison and unshackle our minds. I don't laugh; I stare at them with huge eyes, helpless. They take me gently, in my filthy rags, down the lane. A comrade staggers from the Bride's door, cheek laid open, two fingers awry. I look in: she is prone from the struggle and her head has knocked at the wall's foot, but a smile of sweet surrender is stealing across her face. – "Wait," I tell them, "In a moment she'll be quiet – her lover is coming." She lies there, parting the shreds of her grey shift for her lord.

The young men stare. I stare. For I am dark but the Bride of Christ is fair. Her plump hands cradle the air, her thighs part. We see the fleece below her belly part, and the so wet lips lapping and hugging the true invisible. And she jolts, her body lunges to the hilt of those ghostly thrusts. Oh blessed Bride. I lean back, almost faint, against one of the soldiers. Yes, his mouth is ajar with amazement but, hard against my thigh lies the truth of the matter. My hand goes back to it and eases the lump around till it's flat against his belly. Outside the fabric of his uniform I stroke him swift and gently. The Bride is rising for her release, her body comes up upon her heels from the cell floor, her fingers claw the air, she is thrusting, screaming. My young guard hunkers like a dog against my hand; his chin weighs upon my shoulder; a soft moan escapes him. There, we have soiled his uniform.

Under the wide sky and pigeons tumbling, they douse us from tin buckets in the yard. We clean ourselves at the trough, beside the almond tree. – "So, Lilith, you were right," the Bride smiles. I anoint her shoulders with handfulls of clear water – "What will you do, Bride," I ask, with eyes for my young guard across the cobbles. – "Get far away," she says, "till the times straighten out. And you?" – "Follow the times," I laugh, "I've been waiting." Her eyes are troubled behind her smile – "Well," she sighs, "we are not done with each other yet." – "We'll see," I say. Our hands run over with water, we attend to each other, our hair streams down our shoulders. We dance like grape-treaders, the dark girl and the white woman in the old horse trough. The soldiers grin uncertainly, and one comes over with clothes for us. As we dry ourselves my young guard's eyes rove from my breasts to the Bride's thighs and then, ashamed, to the faces of his comrades.

I am led, white-robed, into the white room. Above and around me in the cold light are the combat jackets and the earnest young faces of the revolution. Faces of the barrio, the village, the suburbs mostly. All transparent. I am the audience: these are a poor lot of mummers. The doctor who has been with me all week brings me forward. She says – "Comrades, this girl – whom we have called Estella for she cannot remember her name – was in the prison cellars, among the violently insane. We do not know how long she had been lying there in filth, abused by her gaolers. There are no records for her and, since she exhibits a classic traumatic amnesia, she can tell us nothing about her background, or when and why she was incarcerated." They could have listened to Lubo – I heard him crying out *Hundreds of years – don't let her out,* before they locked him up in the Bride's old cell.

A young doctor comes over, from the group by the podium, to look at my eyes. He is not like the others, like the ones up there. I read their thoughts: each believes that he could be my salvation, could restore me to my self. In his bed. For, clean in my white robe I am young and unmistakably beautiful. But this man believes in his skill; he scarcely notices me. I want him. He steadies my face gently with his hand, strong but delicate like a woman's, and stares through a steel tube into my left eye. I see the flank of his huge eye turning; I tremble, but his hand is firm. He is shy but sure, his body within his uniform like an unexplored boy's statue. Behind my eyes I dream an awakening for him. When he lowers the instrument, perplexed, I seize his wrists – a little girl, great eyes upon his. I beg him – "Help me, please help me. No one can help me if you will not."

In the carriage I ask what they have done with Christ's Bride. – "Ah yes, you mean the one called Eva. She has been sent to a convent in the hills." He turns to me seriously: "We shall keep some of those places open, you see – so long as they can prove their usefulness. Besides, how could we re-educate the older nuns ...?" Oh don't bore me, my chosen one. What he is hiding is a terrible sadness – I shall take it from him. I start to weep softly. The walls of the old city pass us; we are coming to fields. – "She was your friend?" he asks. I am sobbing now and he puts his arm protectively around me. In the open carriage I throw my arm around his neck. I kiss his throat. He draws back, troubled at himself – "You are a child of nature. We will help you ..." – "I love you," I whisper, "With you I will be safe." My face is an inch from his – his breath is like lemon flowers. My robe is open and he cannot look away.

His house was the police chief's. A carriage gate at the back through the high orchard wall by the stables. – "My wife will be your companion," he tells me as we walk under the fruit trees, "a sister for you." He does not believe this; neither do I. He is becoming ashamed, he shrinks beside me, beginning to walk like a servant. She has a merchant's eyes. She is tall, full-breasted, beautiful. Contempt in her eyes and, for me, hatred. I hear them wrangling through the wall of my room; when he talks to her his voice is higher, pleading. Before dawn he goes down and walks in the orchard – poor love, I am coming. In the stable, upon the carriage seat, I draw him into me. He is in a trance at first, and then his body runs mad, as if he has not had a woman for months. He drenches my breasts with tears and comes to me again and again almost without pause. The leather seat is wet with his release; the orchard air, as the first birds sing, is spiced with his sperm. He moves away and sits in despair upon the running board. Oh my boy, my love, I will save you from all these tears.

She knows without knowing. When he has left for the hospital she sets out to win me. She confides – the big empty doll with beautiful hair and breasts. When things have settled down they

will move to her mother's town – he will practise there. She will
have her own carriage. Her father was the corn chandler, and
mayor too – not all the old ways were bad, she says. Meanwhile this
is a nice house the have been given, though in poor repair – the
government should give them more help. In her kitchen, above the
dresser, is a statue of the Virgin – "Imagine, I must hide her when
officials visit." I am to help her clean up the top floor. Her little
brother will be coming next week – a man must help his relatives.
But Anton (*my* Anton) is not the man her first husband, the mining
agent, was: "*He* was a man with will." She changes her dress twice
in the day, letting me see the body that he has touched, that she can
deny him. Magnificent, yes – the heavy, firm breasts, the ripe
belly. But her thighs are thickening, and I see that her skin is a
snake's.

At dinner she patronises me – our little Estella – and honeys her
words to him. He is distraught and his eyes are for no one. She
takes him off early to bed. I hear her groaning and commanding,
goading that sweet, almost hairless body that is *mine*. He labors; I
can wait.

She cuts aubergines in the kitchen, before the Virgin. –
"Naturally you will be leaving us soon," she says. "There is
nothing much wrong with you. You have suffered, my dear, of
course but that is behind you ..." She slices cabbage, onions. "Some
official will need a housekeeper, just you see, and then one day,
Estella, a man will come who may consider you for a wife –
imagine, your own little kitchen. Don't hope for too much, but
there are some decent men still among the poor." I take the knife
from her. I look into the glazed blue eyes of that Mary doll on the
shelf. I cut cleanly, leisuredly. My love comes in at six o'clock, worn
out from his teaching and his troubles. His dinner is prepared. I go
out to meet him, beneath the pomegranate trees – I have dressed
like a bride for him. I carry her head, swinging from its beautiful
long hair, in my hand.

Anton is weak. He looks at me with horror. He has not stopped
trembling since we finished the grave, and I did most of that work.
He has no appetite. Now he tears at my body with as much hatred
as need. He cannot sleep. To avoid his thoughts he turns back to
me. We are still clinging to each other when dawn comes. – "She
was destroying you," I soothe him. "I saw. She did not marry you
for yourself – you were trapped." – "You have trapped me, you have
destroyed me. ..." The sickening high-pitched tone in his voice. He

goes to work, distracted. I scrub the kitchen. I wear her clothes, pinned and belted, through the house. I go back to their bed and lie with skirts drawn up to caress myself, drawing my fingers across my womb's mouth hungrily, till I tumble into the darkness he could not take me to.

Her brother is a stupid lump. He stares at me; I tell him his sister will be home next week. Anton falls asleep on the couch after dinner, twisting with bad dreams the moment his eyes close. Her brother comes to watch me at the sink – "You're crazy, aren't you?" he says. "What was it like in prison? Did the men do things to you?" – "What would you know about that?" I retort, briskly scouring a pan. I suppose my hips are quivering. His fat mouth smirks – "I know. I'll give you a gold escudo if you let me watch you undress." I laugh. He has got himself excited just talking about it. When I go up and change he comes whistling past my door. I laugh again. We have given him my little room; I make sure he hears us this night.

Anton is lost. I offer him a new life and he trembles at his own thoughts, bolts from his shadow. This morning he could not make love to me, lay moaning like an imbecile, went off to the hospital on foot, looking to right and left as if the birds were informers. I see nothing in him now. The foolish brother stands behind me at the window – "I could tell my sister," he says. – "Tell her then" I shrug. "You're all the same: a nest of guinea pigs." He tags along like a shadow trailing me down to the market and back through the side lanes. He is pestering me the whole time, always a few steps behind me, talking as if to himself. He says monotonously – "Let me touch you. I want to know. You don't know what it's like for me, thinking all the time about it. Won't you let me do it to you? You tease me on purpose. I want to do it; please let me see what it's like." I ignore him, walking ahead with a light step. "Let me, please. I'm not like the others," he pleads, "I won't tell. I'm only waiting till I'm old enough to get free of them." I slip in at the wicket gate and lean back against the wall inside, in the sunlight. He comes shambling by, still droning "My mother's servant let me see her. You don't know what it's like at my age." He stands foolishly, looking around. – "Alright" I say. He turns and gawps, non-plussed. "I said alright, so now what's wrong?" He sets down my vegetable basket, staring, and half steps forward. He suspects a trick. His eyes flick up and down, away from mine. He stands a little clear of me and pulls up his sister's skirt. Clumsy. When the sides of his hand meet my thighs his eyes flare, he is breathing hard through the nose. And I am excited – he doesn't know what to do with that clump of wet hair, but his legs shiver and, see, he has come in his pants. His comical face, as if he had swallowed a spoon. I run laughing up to the house.

I am cutting up a chicken when he comes in with the basket. – "Give me more time," he says, "I want to do it to you. You'll let me, won't you? Look." He doesn't know I can see him anyway in her vanity mirror. Who would have thought that that body could sport such an organ? – it has a huge head with the skin lipping back from it as it rises. I turn, wiping my hands on the apron; they are still slick a little from the meat. He stares from his tool to me and I bend to take him into my mouth. He leans back, gasping, against the table; I can taste the sperm from his jag in the garden. My tongue's tip runs about that little eye and I ease the skin back further, closing my teeth lightly over the cockscomb's ridge. He cannot move now, my tongue is the only free thing. Around and across and strumming the little anchor-string under the head. He is muttering, like a drunken prayer; one leg shakes uncontrollably, his fingers play impromptus on the table edge. I am driving him mad. My right hand works around his sack and it shivers up, shrinking till it is furrowed like a primrose leaf. His moaning is deperately loud in the kitchen. Alright, I relax my teeth and go down with taut, moist lips – down and back and down, down. I pull in my cheeks and trill with my tongue. He falls back on the table as his light spunk comes in little spurts, and swales on my palate. A quick thigh-clench and I, silent, shuddering, am there too.

He seems almost asleep. His eyes half open and close again. I stand watching my creation. When his cheeks and lips, puffed with the ferment of his youth, have tautened, when his shoulders fill out and he learns to walk at ease, he will be beautiful. There must be a purpose for him, if this fog he has breathed all his life can be blown away. Lilith can be generous when the mood is on her. He is watching me, his smile is almost angelic. – "Thank you," he says, sitting up, "Now can I do it to you like Anton does?" I laugh and kiss his brow: – "Oh no – this way you'll remember me better. Now listen, Molo; I've misjudged you. I don't know what you'll become, but you have to get away. Your sister's dead and Anton's going insane. And there's danger afoot, believe me. Go away, get across the border, for a while at least." He buttons his trousers slowly, looking his age again, though when he stands up he is taller than me. "You'll find plenty of real money in your sister's shoe box. And, no – forget me: I'm leaving too, in my own direction." – "But when are you going?" he demands. – "Tonight, maybe in the morning. But you must leave before Anton gets back – get that money and whatever you need while I finish this meal." But he can't leave me. He keeps coming back down into the kitchen and running his hands over me. My breasts fascinate him – it is so comical, curious, without real lust how he stands there looking at the soft mounds in his hands, as if they were not a part of me. And he keeps trying to get his thing into me – I am trying to cook, and we are wrestling around the kitchen, shrieking like eight-year-olds. Once he does get it between my legs when I back against the dresser. The poor blonde Virgin, what she must watch. And the tip of his cock, sliding through the furrow of my wet lips, brings him off again. Not that he has much spunk left. "Nearly," I taunt, slipping around like a matador off the boards; – "I'm still a virgin" he screams in mock dismay – ah he can laugh, he is learning. And of course Anton, sent home from the hospital because he's grown incompetent, comes roaring in, kicking the boy, trying to strangle me. – "Go, Molo," I scream at him, "I'm alright. Get far away." He runs off through the orchard, and doesn't forget to snatch up the little sack with his sister's escudos. Good boy.

Anton is going for the knife. That knife. I move like a fox and grap his arm; I almost break it. – "Think what you like," I say. "Call it the strength of madness if you like, but I could kill you with my hands, so calm down." I slap him hard. "You're going to take me away this minute, up through the pass to Tiralla. Then you can do what you like, I'm finished with all this." He talks as if he were asleep – "Can't do that, the Blues are closing in on us, Raposa is forming an army in the hills, we won't get through. I'm ruined – my reputation, my practice – they despise me ..." – "Why should a eunuch care?" I slap him again. "Get the carriage ready, I'll be down at the stables in five minutes."

I wear one of her mock-peasant dresses. He is shaking so much as we pass the hospital gates that I have to grab the reins. I turn up the steep road for Tiralla – just in time. Patrols are out, they are closing the roads and barricading the city again. The fear of Raposa is in the air, the Blues are coming back for revenge on the liberators. But we see no uniforms on the road, and I get down at the bridge outside Tiralla as dusk floods the pass. He has not spoken the whole way; just drooped and sighed. I throw the reins onto his knees – "Goodbye," I say and set off across the bridge. –

"Why didn't you kill me too?" he calls after me, hoarsely. I shout over my shoulder – "I know about pity. It's not for such as you." I don't like being mistaken.

Far below me the river snarls in its narrow bed. That is the water that feeds the town, the fountains, the horse trough in the prison yard. The moisture which crept whispering down my cell walls had passed this way. I have an appointment in the hills. When I am down the rocky trail, at the river's edge, I walk upstream. The valley forks a mile above the village and the waters of three streams meet. A hunter's moon is nudging its way over the eastern ridge, blood red but fading as it climbs. At the first wide pool I take off my shoes and that grey dress, and throw them out from the flat rocks. The dress streams out in the current and, like a head for its empty neck, the great moon lies there for a moment, beside me in the pool. I move on again, in my shift. Two dogs appear from the bushes, lean hounds, and trot behind in my shadow.

The waters meet with many tangled voices, spreading across a gravel bar, moonwashed. I wade across, the dogs splashing beside me, to the figure that sits on a low rock at the centre. The Bride looks up: – "And the little doctor, Lilith?" how her voice carries on the darkness. I stand above her: "And the old nuns, Bride?" She smiles sadly, looking down and pushing at the gravel with her toes. The white dog and the black, myself and the Bride. She kisses me full on the lips as I bend to her. Our eyes are open, shifting like moons as we move against each other. Every particle of our flesh is awake and touching in the atom dance. No man has this. No man would remember if he did. I slip down the Bride's white body, my lips tugged by her skin, and kneel in the water. My head rests for a moment below her breasts while my hands fall slowly from her shoulders, along her body to her thighs. I crouch, my mouth opens and closes upon those secret lips, my tongue tracing the precious, hooded flesh. Here, at the centre, Lilith prays and drinks at the gate of heaven and hell, and the moon pours down the body of the Bride and across my shoulders. Her essence flows out through her hands into the stream, and the waters flow into me where I kneel. The dogs stand tied in the moonlight; the rippling shadows lie. Through her tears the Bride calls my name: – "I think we are coming to the end ..." – "In our own ways," I whisper, too low for her to hear, and then, aloud, "Tomorrow," I say, "or the next day."

They are looting in the village. Houses are thatched with flame, the air is seasoned with smoke and wine. At each new horror the

screams fly up as if it were a firework display. Here and there the
Blues are running in groups, dropping one pile of loot for a better,
kicking in doors. And the farmers cluster like cattle, watching the
spectacle of their own destruction. The Bride has been lying this
week in peasant beds, learning the crude refueling of the earth.
Tomorrow she will die, as that woman by the mud wall is being
killed now: raped, torn, forgotten.

The woman's daughter stands helpless, watching, her hands
fallen by her sides. I call her to me – she would obey any command,
now that her mother has stopped screaming. I take her hand, my
white hound licks her fingers. We walk in silence away from the
burning houses towards the ridge. Only the moon sees the woman,
the child and the two dogs under the hill. But below the next pass a
Blue patrol comes running out with lights and backs us against the
stones. They are not so drunk, and no better for that. Two of them
come for me slowly, hands poised, as if stalking a rabbit which
might suddenly bolt. The child has learnt well, she tries to break
free from me. I hold her hand firmly, – "It's Raposa I'm here to see,"
I tell them. "Where do I find him?" They hesitate; one in the group
behind laughs: – "What would Raposa want with a woman!" They
start forward again; my dogs bare their teeth. "I'll be happy to tell
him your opinion," I say. The nearest man, with insignia on his
sleeve, takes me by the shoulder, doubtfully. – "So you know
Raposa?" – "Why else would I be here? I've travelled a great
distance to find him." – "You look wrong," he says. "If you're lying
you know what will happen." – "If I'm not lying *you* know what will
happen." He tells two of his men to go with me – "But first ..." he
runs his hands down my front and thighs, knowing hands, "in case
of weapons," he smiles. He takes his time: "I hope you are lying."

I stand in the tent door. He is forty years old perhaps. Lean,
clean-shaven, expressionless. Discipline has tightened his full
lips, hooded his eyes. His aide, dismissed, ducks past me glaring.
Raposa watches me, as I him. He is not what the stories say – a
controlled intelligence informs his whole body; around him is a
pale aura of detachment, the world does not touch him. I have been
so often deceived, but this man is different. He nods towards the
child: – "Your daughter?" – "She is from the village. Your men
were killing her mother when I found her." His eyes tighten: –
"They are *canaille*, dogs," he shrugs, "don't trouble me with this."
– "I did not intend to," my eyes work through that aura, touching
him. For a moment he believes he has known me before, has

glimpsed me at the rim of a dream; a strange humor enters his eyes, and then his voice: – "So what do you want from me?" – "Only a safe conduct to take this child to Mesita. Then I'll come back." He sits on a canvas chair in one clean movement and leans back; the pale eyes come up to mine: – "Why would you do that?" – "I want to be with you." His eyes drift past my shoulder; he laughs shortsly: – "Go away," he says. "Yes, you may have safe-conduct for what it is worth, but don't come back." I let the silence hang till he looks back at me. – "Why did you pretend to know me?" I ask softly. His fox eyes, used to penetrate and confuse men, fence with mine. – "It was unusual; I was curious. That is sufficient reason." – "And now," I say, "you are less curious? You are not wondering, as I am?" He turns to his camp desk, busying himself at once with the half-made map there. His pen scratches, he speaks as he works: – "My brother goes up for supplies in two hours. He will take you." And then "You have a nerve that I like." – "That is sufficient reason," I smile.

I sit behind the driver of the wagon, next to Cabro. How could he have come from the same womb – this one so massive, bearded, looming at the world? – "What is this with my brother?" he demands. "What does he want with a slut like you?" The jolting of the wheels throws us against each other; I draw away. He sneers "I saw you when you came into the camp. So he has found you a pretty dress, and shoes: you look even more a tart ... You're my sort of woman – my brother does not look at women." He reaches over and grasps my thigh with his huge fingers; I push him away. He laughs and spits into the night.

We go on through the half-darkness, bumping up the road in the moonlight. The wagon swings like a hammock from side to side. The child sleeps upon empty sacks, the dogs at her feet, and I move back and lie beside her. The stars swing through the canvas flap, the driver talks softly to the horses. Cabro's hand wakes me, sliding firmly over my hip. I turn to push him off. – "Ah you won't refuse me," he growls. "We understand each other." His hand is inside my dress, dwarfing the breast that he toys with roughly. I turn back again: – "Don't wake the child," I whisper. The hand moves down and spreads across my belly, pressing me against him to the point almost of pain. He obliterates me: this hand and the weight of his arm on my side are as intimate with death as with love. The dress his brother found me is open down the front, my shift torn through. He pulls up my clothes with his right hand and I arch myself to help him, feeling his body now against my back –

dense hair, a man's belly. Like a bull's, his organ is small but it presses hard at me from behind and butts between my thighs. His fingers stroke me rapidly, as if he were touching himself, spreading the weeping lips of my womb's mouth, while the heel of his palm stays pressed, dizzyingly, upon my mound. I pull my knees up almost to my belly, and his legs follow mine, nesting against me. The horn-like arch of his sex is inside me, and we lie for long minutes, not moving, while the jolting, swaying wagon floor stirs us together into a rapture. The tension is too great – greedy and commanding, he starts to move in me with swift, short strokes, his belly pressing upon my buttocks, his coarse beard rushing at my ear. His hand bears down again at my groin – I am going away with him. I reach out to grip something and find the child's hand. Her eyes open and fix upon mine. As his body arches in three last thrusts that almost lift me from the floor, I cry out laughing in a forgotten tongue and she smiles. Cabro turns at once onto his back. – "I feel better about things now," he says, staring up at the swaying canvas roof, "If there's any trouble I'll just tell Raposa what I know of you." – "Leave the thinking to your brother," I say, "No one will deceive him but himself." But Cabro is asleep already. The child is singing to herself.

It is still not light when they drop us at the edge of the woods. Cabro gives me three hours – "Why don't you stay up here?" he grumbles as he lifts the child down to me. "It would suit me, and there'll be no place for a woman down there tomorrow." But he grins as I turn to go – he knows I'll be back.

We go up past the ruins, the pine-mist swimming around us. The child lets go of my hand and runs ahead with the dogs, catching at their bright collars. Above her the morning star is the only sign as the night fades. The changeless place: the fallen, petrified tree by the old well and, as I approach, out of the mist step the sisters. They wait for me at the source. Naked, I step down into the well and lie in the water, my head against my mother's knees, while her sister stands knee-deep and pours the bright water over me, dipping it up in a bowl of silver. The dogs lap at the pool across from me and the child comes down the low steps and stands with the water around her ankles. My mother strokes my hair: – "What is it, Lilith, have you grown tired at last?" I tell her no, but I must step down and leave the child in my place. – "Then you *are* weary." – "Not that, Mother – just that I choose to start a new thing in the world." –

"You must not hope for anything new," she warns, but her sister leaves off her work and says gently – "She is her own mistress." I step from the pool, up onto the grass, and when I am dressed I call the child to me. I stoop and kiss her gravely on the lips; her little mouth returns the pressure. I shiver, as though a hand reached into me and touched something hidden there. This sadness – poor men, poor women. She turns and goes trustingly to my Aunt, taking her hand. She is the last to fade into the mist, the dogs beside her. I walk towards the sunrise; when I look back there is only the morning star above the ridge, undimmed even in the light of day.

Seventeen crows hang on the hill wind, shouting as I turn down the valley. The mist blows out in shreds from the trees into the sunlight and there, below, is the Blues' encampment, silent in the dawn and far smaller than the rumors told. Cabro overtakes me, easing the wagon only slightly on the steep track so that I have to run and reach up for him to haul me aboard. – "I thought you had taken my advice," he grunts and then, patting the carbine by his knee, "you'll wish you had, by tomorrow." He rests his arm casually round my waist, but no more, and as the wagon jogs slowly down, his eyes stare out keenly through the short hours towards death.

A mounted figure, with a riderless horse. Raposa waits at the last fork, erect, contained, not moving as Cabro gets down and goes to him. Like a hawk overlooking a bear he sits calmly, speaking brief words with his eyes on the distance. I melt inside, I understand; there is no one like him in the world. I want him. I walk to him; his eyes pass swiftly, with a glint of intelligence, across my face and shoulders; he bends to hand me the spare reins. I pull myself up, hoisting my skirts to straddle the gelded bay. Cabro's eyes follow my legs thoughtfully, but Raposa has already moved off to the North and I pull the rein over and follow.

The narrow track climbs steeply to the mesa that looks over the city. The bridles ring, the horses spurn small stones down the hillside, we climb in silence for an hour. He unbuttons his tunic for the heat: his skin is tawny, his ribs show lightly. Round his neck, on a cord, hangs a rough piece of metal. I yearn towards that body as though I had created it. He lifts me from the saddle, his hands beside my breasts, his pale hazel eyes sardonic upon mine. I touch his skin wonderingly and finger his pendant: – "What is it?" He lifts back the tunic – beneath his heart is a white scar, puckered and indenting: – "They dug the bullet out of me." We walk to the cliff's edge.

He is a priest without faith, an artist without vision. "You are a gambler, then," I tell him. – "Finally, perhaps. Meanwhile I simply watch ..." – "Yet you have power ..." – "Merely to deflect boredom." – "I want you," I say, to myself, to him. – "I am an observer," he repeats. I dance for him on the edge of the world, my bare feet bruising the wild thyme. I float in a cloud of spice and indolence, the South Wind lifting and moulding my clothes against me. I dance to old rhythms of self-love and offering, along the bluffs before him, to where the ridge turns North again. And I see, as I dip and spin back towards him, a lancing flash of metal in the distance. A line of soldiers winds through the pass – the Reds come down from the North for my beloved's blood; the city will not fall. I dance back and run to him, falling exhausted and laughing against him. He holds me, lifts my face to his in a cool, utterly passionless kiss. I am close to fainting with desire and joy. – "I love you," I breathe. He draws away from me.

I who have known a patience more dense than history, seethe with unrest in the dreamy light of the tent. The breath of grass drying and canvas bear in deliciously upon me, but fiercely I will the evening to come. Through the day's heat, as the Reds close in upon this camp where the soldiers idle intensely, preparing to kill or to die, I follow my love's command and wait for his coming. I have prepared a couch for him of sacks and uniforms, hedged round with ammunition crates, and here in my shift I lie, teasing myself through the afternoon, teased by the limping hours. For he has said that he will come to me, this night before the battle; saying – "You may bring ill-luck" as we rode into camp through the staring men "but my own follies entertain me above all others." My love, your fortune is out of my hands, but you are everything to me. Time coils itself towards our consummation.

Will he not come? It is dusk already, the fires throw shapes over this tent and I have no light. The ambush is hours away only, there is little time. Then – "Come," he says from his doorway. I gesture to the bed, he ignores me. "Everything's ready: we ride down to the city at dawn. Now you and I," he says, "we shall walk through the camp unrecognised. Always I do this before a fight." He throws a cloak around my shoulders; it laps upon my feet.

Caverns of fire and night. The mouths of tents and the eyes of men lit from below, the reek of wine and roasting flesh, the laughter and songs of the doomed. Circles of hazard where hands like claws tumble knaves and kings in the dust, and pawn themselves against tomorrow's chance. Two soldiers squat, faces etched by flame and sensuality, preening the swelling cock's necks between their thighs; thirty men breathe as one in the low ring, and break together into cries and curses as the birds are released. The cocks dance, catching the light; they leap and spin, driving spurs and beaks into each other's pride, trampling blindly, till one falls slack and pulsing on the earth, blood leaking from its eye, and the victor crows. The sparks fly up in the night, a befuddled village girl gags on a fat man's prick while his comrades anoint her with brandy and wine. My love is alert, like a hawk on the wrist, attuned to the camp's heart, guiding me through the tents with his hand strong on my shoulder. We pass the sentries unnoticed and walk towards the river.

Where is the moon? The hills have held her back. Pale on the grass lies the naked body of the Bride, her eyes on the stars, wine on her thighs and sperm across her cheeks. Her dead lips speak to me, there is laughter in the voice, but all I catch is my name, once, twice.

Raposa looks over the water: – "It feels as it should," he says. "Tomorrow our flag will fly on the cathedral." The frogs are clamoring around the backwater, the lilies gleam white and yellow on the black pool. He slips the cloak from my arms and trails it on the grass – I throw myself on it and spread it, turning to face him as he kneels beside me, the lost constellations over his shoulder. He leans to me, taking his weight upon his hands, brushing his lips across my cheek-bones, around my eyelids. Low cries escape me, beyond my control; I want him, I want him. His mouth nestles under my ear, his hand at last reaches my breast. I crook my arm round his neck, urging him towards me, guiding his mouth to mine. My mind is empty for a moment, the night dissolves, and he is kneeling again above me, between my legs, easing his arms from the tunic. My hands flutter upon my belly, tugging at my hem. His fingers come down upon mine, his thumb lingers on my navel and the earth gasps with me. He is naked now in the starlight – his pale body, the dark pointer of his manhood. I half rise to reach for him. His hand parts my sex and traces the moisture up my body, circling the tips of my breasts. I fall back, his face upon mine, and he guides himself into me. Simple man and simple woman, coupling beside the water, under the turning sky. My feet kick up at the stars and then lock him within me, his aura, his strength. We move like a small wave rippling upon the field. He is silent, I am clamoring for completion; and there, a fraction behind me, he comes, and the wave breaks into me. – "Oh my love, my love," I cry, watching the stars, unlocking my treacherous womb.

Afterword

Two titles in this collection need acknowledgement.

"*Dusty Bluebells*" is a children's street-song, heard commonly in Ireland's Six Counties. Davey Hammond used it as the title of his heartbreaking film documentary about Falls Road kids in the 1970's. I obviously stole it from him.

No one could use the title "*Lilith*," without acknowledging that a great book by that name already exists. Except for one chapter (which W.H. Auden called "shymaking"), George Macdonald's "*Lilith*" is a masterpiece: the first great fantasy novel, without which Kipling and Tolkien (and their degenerate offspring) could not have existed. Macdonald's "*Lilith*" is, however, Christian and redemptive. Mine is not.

And while I'm at it (since popular songs form one of the wefts of this book) I should acknowledge that Jackson Browne made a record called "*Running on Empty*."

With the story, "*Snake Oil*," I have a moral problem. My aesthetic is one of transmutation, not transcription, yet "*Snake Oil*" is based on an actual atrocity which occurred in Guatemala in 1982, and gets some of its force from that fact. For several years I read the story at public readings but would not publish it. Then the Catholic ecumenical magazine, *Grail*, asked for it. I gave permission, prefacing the story with this paragraph:

There is no political system, yet, which does not countenance some cruelty and injustice. But the central incident in *Snake Oil* involves a refined brutalisation that is, to me, symptomatic of life under right-wing oligarchies, specifically those that have flourished, and still flourish, in

171

Central and South America. It is a near-documentary account of what happened in a Guatemalan village in 1982. Sandro the Magician (or, if you prefer, Charlatan) is of course my invention. He is the oblique lens through which an artist, as opposed to propagandist, must scrutinise evil. The pressures on Sandro are the pressures on us all.

I believe the editors of *Grail* sent my royalty to the Nicaraguan Minister of Education.

I will not accept any money for "*Snake Oil.*" A proportion of any royalties from this collection will be set aside. The sum will probably be laughable, but if it ever amounts to anything it will be used to get some Guatemalan kid out of an orphanage and into a (Guatemalan) family.

Some of these stories have appeared in *Exile, Grail, The New Quarterly*, and the anthology, *Rainshadow.*